FOUR QUARTETS

Four
Quartets

Poetry in the Pandemic

EDITED BY
KRISTINA MARIE DARLING
& JEFFREY LEVINE

TUPELO PRESS
2020

Four Quartets: Poetry in the Pandemic
Introductions and compilation copyright © 2020 Tupelo Press. All rights reserved.

ISBN 978-1-946482-45-7 (hb)
ISBN 978-1-946482-44-0 (pb)

Design by adam b. bohannon.
Cover image by B. A. Van Sise.
Copyright © 2020. Used with permission of the artist.

First paperback edition: November 2020
First hardcover edition: November 2020
Library of Congress Catalog-in-Publication data available upon request.

Tupelo Press
P.O. Box 1767
North Adams, Massachusetts 01247
(413) 664-9611 / Fax: (413) 664-9711
editor@tupelopress.org / www.tupelopress.org

Tupelo Press is an award-winning independent literary press that publishes fine fiction, non-fiction, and poetry in books that are a joy to hold as well as read. Tupelo Press is a registered 501(c)(3) non-profit organization, and we rely on public support to carry out our mission of publishing extraordinary work that may be outside the realm of the large commercial publishers. Financial donations are welcome and are tax deductible.

With boundless gratitude to the following for their generous support of this project:

Joseph P Morra

Gary Granberg

Richard Ridout Osler

Dawn McGuire

AE Hines

CONTENTS

FOREWORD

For these past many months, every single one of us—every living being the world over—has been living with a pandemic the likes, the breadth and reach of which, not one of us has ever experienced, save maybe those very few who were alive for the "Spanish" flu of 1918. We have been sheltering at home and social distancing outside, watching as an incoming tide of masks literally remakes the faces of every country on earth. We've been out of work, out of play, and in so many ways, out of luck. The U.S. alone has taken an astonishing brunt of COVID-19, and as of this writing, we've lost a heartrending more than 200,000 of our neighbors, and have suffered 5.8+ million cases. By the time you read this, those numbers will be significantly higher. Utterly staggering numbers.

Here, at the approach of autumn, many of our states continue to see record numbers of our countrywomen and men falling ill, even as our health-care workers daily (and nightly) march into the heart of the nightmare. Yet, there are as many stories of triumph and hope as there are of despair and loss.

We know (because they tell us) that writers everywhere here and around the globe are trying to make sense of things, not just of the unspeakable virus itself, not just of its terrible financial toll, but also of another unprecedented aspect of our historical moment, as we see and participate in a grassroots movement toward social and racial justice, ignited by one after another casual, heartless murder of a Black American by formerly impervious cops. All the while, we find ourselves suffering through the cruelest, most sadistic, most narcissistic "administration" in the life of our country. Our great national experiment in democracy is in grave danger.

What we writers do, then, is bear witness. When we put out a call to poets to send us what they've been writing, it was like relieving a pressure valve. We invited 12 transcendent poets each to send us short folios of pandemic-related work, and we have had our hair blown back by the beauty and power of what they've sent us.

> But to stand & witness what makes us
> afraid, no, I can't take any praise
> for god-given lust of the eye, true
>
> nature of being human, though we
> onlookers may be condemned or blessed
> to gaze long enough to see clearly...
> YUSEF KOMUNYAKAA & LAREN MCCLUNG
> quartet fragment

Then we sent an open call to poets everywhere to let us read what they've been writing, and in two months more than 1,000 poets responded with their own 12-page folios, many of them equally transcendent. Of those, we selected four more astonishing folios to round out our anthology, the one you're holding now.

> my mind drives back
> north to the hospital, where each
> precast concrete parking structure
> is named after a flower.
> DORA MALECH
> quartet fragment

It is a privilege for us to present these folios to you, each one in its own way life affirming, at a time when affirmation is itself our balm and salvation.

Lord,
during this period of quarantine
and social distancing,
let me swirl my poetic concoction
and brew up an elixir
that'll mount an attack on ignorance
and enlighten the disbelievers.

> JIMMY SANTIAGO BACA
> quartet fragment.

Here at Tupelo Press we have devoted 22 years to publishing life-changing work in beautifully made books. From the start, we've wanted to champion both emerging and established writers from diverse ethnic and cultural backgrounds. We've made a central part of our mission an undertaking to provide a platform for writers of color, for the LGBTQ, immigrant, and Native American communities, and for women writers, whose work constitutes two out of every three books we print.

During the pandemic, I listened.

> RICK BAROT
> quartet fragment

In the spirit of a new consciousness throughout the country, from this day forward we pledge to redouble our commitment to provide writers of color, LGBTQ voices, immigrant writers, and Native American writers a place to stand and be heard.

When I feel hampered simply to lace my shoes to go outside,

saying, "Today will be the day I'll make a difference," when,
finally, it occurs to me, *I have some time on my hands,*

I pull it together

trying my best to imitate the sun ...
A. VAN JORDAN
quartet fragment

Kristina Marie Darling & Jeffrey Levine
TUPELO PRESS

FOUR QUARTETS

Poetic Prayer

JIMMY SANTIAGO BACA

JIMMY SANTIAGO BACA's poetry titles include *Healing Earthquakes* (2001), *C-Train & 13 Mexicans* (2002), *Winter Poems Along the Rio Grande* (2004), and *Spring Poems Along the Rio Grande* (2007). In addition to the American Book Award, Baca has received a Pushcart Prize and the Hispanic Heritage Award for Literature. Baca has conducted writing workshops in prisons, libraries, and universities across the country for more than 30 years. In 2004 he launched Cedar Tree, a literary nonprofit designed to provide writing workshops, training, and outreach programs for at-risk youth, prisoners and former prisoners, and disadvantaged communities.

Dedicated to Cristina Mormorunni and
the Wildlife Conservation Society's Rocky Mountain Program

Poetic Prayer

Lord,
during this period of quarantine
and social distancing,
let me swirl my poetic concoction
and brew up an elixir
that'll mount an attack on ignorance
and enlighten the disbelievers.

1.
Buffalo Prayer

Prairie flowers bloom
in hoof ruts
in depressed traces in the grass
visible where we
               once roamed;
feels good to go forward,
feels good to give to the two-leggeds,
to trample what separates us, stampede
religious beliefs with the beauty of ourselves—
               we left trails
               for you to follow—
hoof scratch, grip-gash, pinch-push
our ancient hieroglyphic scripture in the dirt,
inscribe on mother's body
our ministry of love and surrender...
               we left trails
               for you to follow.

2.

Buffalo Dance

Heat the prairie,
hooves engrave it
agitate the air, sky, earth
            with a coming,
with heat made hooves
heat-hooves sure as flames
sure as hot red coals
sure as orange/yellow and red
                  buffalo
heart blows the energy of fire
mixed with stars and sun
                  blows
huffs warmth on the world
ribs skull horns hooves
embrace the air, the earth, the light
strenuous tendon fibers
bones and muscle crackle
cracking whatever lays between
                  to remind us one
black snouts and teeth trailed
with bits of wild carrots/blueberries/prairie grass
vegetal peelings,

hooves so hot
chisel air with crystal waves
that blur us
to water and fire alive
                  in the ceremony of living
as dancer to flute
so hoof to earth

breathe   breathe   breathe

rolling into the storm
                    they come
awakening us in the grace of being
in the music of their drum-beating hooves
shaping us into our humanity
carving us back to our prairie-self
with the message
respect, be conscious, listen

we are brothers, sisters,
more heat, more hoof, more breath
                    more heart
hoof music heats us back
to our essence, to our nature of light
to our nature of wind and rain
                            to the fire
from where we come,
                    to the spirit
                    we share.

3.
Buffalos

All over the city
I hear the
explosive sounds
rat-tat-rat-boom—and—nostrils blowing
chest-huffs-heaving
                    Buffalo are coming
shuddering air, dust trails
smoke across sky
spreading dirt clouding the air,

streams over housetops
obscures skyscrapers and stars,
TVs flicker then fuzz
disrupt Netflix movies making mindless fools
grab guns and shoot away, grab knives and slice,
clubs and bludgeon and bombing,
                    Buffalo are coming
furry, bulky bodies avalanche
hooves thunder rubbling pavement
crack streets, toppling street lights,
hemorrhaging traffic, exits jammed,
Martial Law is declared
armored military goon-squads in Bradley tanks
roam the night
with orders to kill the four-hoofed creature, but

                    Buffalo are coming
down the Appalachia trail and Continental Divide
grinding false patriots beneath typhoon hooves
stampeding metal weapons, money, power
                    Buffalo are coming
across the Grand Canyon, splashing
over Niagara Falls,
spanning one end of the world to the other
                    Buffalo are coming
smashing homes and hearts,
waking people, stirring them to think
to feel again, to do away with profit margins,
                    Buffalo are coming
in New Mexico, where I am, I see them
friends call they see them too—
New Hampshire woods, Seattle shoreline,
India's mountaintops,
                    Buffalo are coming

cross deserts and Kansas corn fields
cross Alabama football fields,
Florida golf courses, Southern California beaches,
flattening New York City gyms, crushing
treadmills, stationary bicycles and elliptical machines.

And as the sun rises over the cliffs and on my cabin,
here I am, lying on my side
I watch the sun hit a distant peak,
slowly it comes into sight—emerges from dusk,
then it's time to get up
and get the day's chores done.

But this morning
           a White Buffalo
stands visible in the Autumn mist, and I dash out,
it approaches me in my pasture and I give it a slap
on the rump and it bolts off
through forest trees
and watching it, I have a desire to follow,
answer its call—
its voice spoke to me the way fire talks to darkness

           Get on with lighting you up, it said,
gristle and knees, shoulders and neck,
stomach and fingers, its voice spread throughout me,
one beautiful smooth spreading of light,
           live as a human
           live as human
           live as human.

I Start Thinking

Waiting in line at Whole Foods,
masked and gloved
imagine having names
like
Avocado/
Organic Bread/
Seedless Grapes/
Boneless Chuck Roast/

> they enrapture me,
> make me want their names:

Call me, if you see me walking down the street,
Hey, Avocado! What are you doing?

And I reply,
Naw, same old same Organic Bread,
You wanna mix it up tonight at the new beat-club
Maybe spread up some style jams ...

And he replies,
Maybe invite Seedless, you know,
That boy can mash up the grapes baby ...

And don't forget Boneless
Chuck Roast
Anybody mess with us he be
Putting his weight on them ...

Yeah, okay, I reply,
Get the crew
And let's cook it up...
Ya, we'll stew it up...

My Prayer to the Buffalo

Gentle heart you are,
                    I would say
Sumo-sweetness, the prairie breeze
so bracing it recalls your soul
to times you ambled in amber citrus fields down south,
                    where fragrant fields
nose black as a grape
dangle upward on a vine of wind
enjoying the scent of red, orange and yellow,
                    your heart
                    tenderly folding around the afternoon
                    like fresh corn leaves
                    wrapping a tamale.

Gentle heart you are,
                    Four Directions open to you
                    your prickly scruff fur
                    rough as pineapple skin,
                    the yellow in your eye
                    mango soft,
                        you offer yourself
                        to the Four Directions,
        to all
                    who are hungry,
even those who had forgotten the sacred language of Respect,
who had forgotten the sacred ceremony of Living,
who came and slaughtered and upset the balance,

                    unprotected,
Gentle heart that you are,
first cutting, second cutting, third cutting
each successive generation got thinner and thinner

until you almost became extinct,
                          but The People remembered
                          how children called you Big Leaf,
                          how adults remembered you were
  called Full Beauty,
how the medicine men and healer women
                          took Four Drops Of Blood from you
                          and mixed them with dirt
from Four Directions,
  then they prayed,
  they prayed, prayed prayed
  standing all night on a mountain, in a prairie, at a forest, by
  the shore,
  they prayed they prayed they prayed,

                          until Your Gentle Heart unfolded
                          its leaves again, giving off a
peppery mintiness on the breeze
                          and The People Danced
                          practiced Your Old Ways,
                          sang Your Songs,
                          made You Gifts,
cared again for the land,
told stories around the fire again, grandfather to father to child
and again you multiplied,
                          pizza and soda pops and cornbread
were brought
                          to the pow-wows, eggs, almonds,
piñons,
                          even English muffins & white bread,
                          and La Gente ate and danced and
sang in thanks
                          that Gentle Hearts roamed among
them again.

Buffalo Rain

Strong rain—big, hard masculine drops
smack the canyon forest pines. I hear
a black-nostril'd heave, sigh over the fields.

In the meadow beyond my cabin
Buffalo rain grazes in the morning mist,
nibbles withered grasstips,
wrenches at the day-moon
hanging in dew on twigs—

The Buffalos clomp
over the once-new 2x4's,
(I was going to use building the dog pen,
blackened by a year's weather in the weeds.)

A Hopi friend tells me
gnarly white ginger roots
I'm planting this year,
are buffalo-spirit hooves,
that dig at earth until it thaws through
to release
barrel-chested healthy nubs.

I think of this as I watch
Buffalo rain
in the same meadows
kids from the village
brought O'Keeffe to,
where she found the colors she dreamed of
for her painting.

The children told her what each flower was,
its medicinal and ceremonial use,
how the petals sweep
the blue from sky and save the sky in roots/petals—
(imagine saving sky . . . the way you do pennies in a jar!),
they taught her Chicano/Indio names,
instructed her in the ways of grandmothers
distilling pigments from blossoms and stems.
Without them, there'd be no O'Keeffe paintings
as we know them.

In the 1850s the village was a trading post
where Hopis, Utes, Apaches, Comancheros
Kiowa, Dene, a few Crow and Lakota
traded captives and horses,
a village (not a pueblo), Mexicans
and Indios married, and today we have more tribes
living side by side than anywhere else.

They say O'Keeffe painted the cliffs
behind my cabin and sold the canyon series
for millions to the Kemper museum in Kansas City.
Made her famous and wealthy,
while the villagers were given oranges
and thought they were eating tiny suns.

The same cliffs
I pray to each morning, same cliffs my ancestors
appear each night in ghost form, dancing and praying.
I see them when I go hiking,
two-hundred-year-old young couples sitting in boulders
scooped out by centuries of rain, kissing.
Meet my uncle spirit hunters in other boulders

carved out with stone chisels,
sit in and wait for elk or turkey to come by.
In some boulders chiseled by wind,
young warriors perch as lookouts
for raiding parties.
Some rocks have been whittled smooth
to divert rainwater to gather in pools.

I visit these sacred places and pray, drink the water,
nod to my ancestors—tios, tias, abuelo/as y padres,
see them as clearly as I do my hand.

I thank them for permitting me to be here.

Each morning I ask them for guidance.
Each morning I offer my heart to them.

Later, I catch the morning news,
where viral hornets are swarming cities—
                    Nature, I think,
self-correcting what we haven't,
balancing people out of whack,
arrives to clean house.

    Gives Mother Earth a reprieve from our greed.
Pollution decreases. Traffic lessens. Power Mongers
pause grunting at the trough—
no more maddening gotta-have gotta-do,
no more gluttonous consumption of oil,
no more guzzling consumers,
—not a nuclear bomb or White Dictator
that's come to destroy,
but a tiny invisible microscopic
                    Leveler,
                    Balancer—

we expected Brown People, Chicanos & Mexicans,
we caged them, separated families, murdered them;
we imagined them wielding weapons—drugs, alcohol, bombs,
they warned us these would be the enemy
but an aerial corona star appears in the blood
to settle the books,
empty every commercial establishment,
force humans to cower behind locked doors.

The enemy didn't come at us crossing borders,
swinging machetes and machine guns.
A benign emperor embracing us in groups and crowds,
merging into our breathing, in his glittering carriage, came.

Far from the closest person,
I've only spoken a few words to in thirty years,
in this womb of cliffs
silence is the language I speak,
suspends its mist over everything—

I stand on the porch
listening to the raindrops
tick the green galvanized roof.

Some leaves
didn't fall this winter,
clutter the boughs
still trying to clutch on to Spring,
to what they had,
to what they were, and their failure's
meaning of life
is to surrender—
nothing holds on to what it had,
to what it was.

Gust-clusters strong enough to shove me back,
hackle the crackly beige leaves,
make Bella (my Corso) turn
searching animal movement,
catching a whiff, she lunges tonguelong
growling after ancestral spirits that kindle the air,
tracking their glittering with sniffs
over boulders into the weeds,
dashing up a wildlife trail,
baptized by brush
sparkling rain over her.

I watch
and the silence whispers:
Do not hold on to what you had, Jimmy,
to who you were.
          Live light.

The Time of Gardens

When the Coronavirus hit
Leo, the toothless hound
could no longer pick up aging women
at the gym and shortly after had a nervous breakdown,

hustlers on street corners sold toilet paper
instead of drugs
and the rate of addiction went way down,

neighbors wearing Make America Great Again hats
ordered truckloads of rocks
and built fences and walls to keep the virus out,

the birthrate went way down

rich liberals installed titanium seatbelts
in their Teslas to strap in their tea-cup poodles

(and even, it was heard, mother viruses
had micro-seatbelts installed in their colonies
telling with delight their children viruses
that it was going to get real crazy
since most Americans were unprepared for shit
that was going to hit the fan, so, strap in sweeties!

Also, viral baby-strollers sold out,
as viral births were in the gadzillions
and Viruses celebrated
in their human hosts—think of Brazil's Carnival,
and multiply that by a trillion trillion trillion viruses
feasting and dancing on the human immune system!)

schools closed
for the first time in memory
kids were happy as freed prisoners,

people showing up in emergency rooms
with no bed-capacity
watched Netflix on their mobile phones
and slept on each other,

the homeless lined sidewalks
wrapped in toilet paper to keep warm,
had nice, clean warm butts,

no one took the holy wafer at Sunday mass
and no one went to hell,

grass grew green, flowers bloomed,
dogs sunned comfortably on patios
and since gatherings were banned
and travel discouraged, people could be seen
reading books again,

public health services were dismally lacking
or non-existent (our leader-in-chief had gone into hiding)
and people learned to take care
of themselves, eating right, meeting neighbors,
walking and hiking again,

and what's crazy about all of this? When the wealthy
got on their jets and yachts and hid on their private islands,
gangster viruses hunted them down and took them out—
I mean, how radical is that, right?

it was almost like, in the midst of the pandemic crises
people remembered they were human, had time to think
again, had time to spend with kids,
had time to evaluate their lives and the choices
they made, and change came about, they realized
the jobs they had were wasting their time
the money they spent on tuition and malls and prescriptions
were not needed,

and slowly, the people came out into the sun
and laughed, as if some great enlightenment
had befallen the population, and citizens everywhere,
even prisoners in prison, started writing letters
asking for forgiveness,
people tried to find each other on FB,
shovels came out of sheds
and soon gardens were spreading where before
there were only dirt lots,

and believe it not, buffalos appeared
in parks to graze—

it was a time, future generations would later call,
the time of gardens.

from Trading Riffs
to Slay Monsters

YUSEF KOMUNYAKAA &
LAREN MCCLUNG

YUSEF KOMUNYAKAA's books of poetry include *Dien Cai Dau; Neon Vernacular,* for which he received the Pulitzer Prize; *Warhorses; Emperor of Water Clocks*; and *Everyday Mojo Songs of Earth* (forthcoming from FSG). His honors include the William Faulkner Prize (Université Rennes, France), the Ruth Lilly Poetry Prize, and the 2011 Wallace Stevens Award. His plays, performance art, and libretti have been performed internationally and include *Saturnalia, Wakonda's Dream, Testimony,* and *Gilgamesh.* He teaches at New York University.

LAREN MCCLUNG is the author of a collection of poems, *Between Here and Monkey Mountain* (Sheep Meadow Press), and editor of the anthology *Inheriting the War: Poetry and Prose by Descendants of Vietnam Veterans and Refugees* (W. W. Norton). Her poems have appeared in *Harvard Review, Poetry, Yale Review, Boston Review,* and elsewhere. She teaches at New York University.

At the start of the pandemic, I wrote nine lines (three tercets) and asked Laren to write a response in three tercets. This correspondence of improvisations has continued throughout this historic time and the poetic dialogue has been led by the sway of language, the movement of two minds at play, and the nature of this unfolding moment.

YUSEF KOMUNYAKAA

from Trading Riffs to Slay Monsters

Now, let's go back far as we dare
to go, back to that land bridge
made of untrusting earth & ice,

to a boorish faith in our rhythm
of footsteps, the fleeting mantra
of wordless dreams, long before

there were stories & breathless
myths to pass down through the
brutal ages, to a blinding sunset.

Dig down deep below the ice
where spores of flora & fauna
once bloomed, devil's tongue

& carrion flower lured dung beetles
to the gods' nectar to thrive
in a rainforest long gone now.

Yes, you'll have to go back before
the upright body to remember
the scent of canopy & swampy soil.

True, it is hard to believe the miasma
they slushed through in thorny gullies
of berry mush hundreds of rotted years,

& then the fiery dark ooze of tar pits.
Some turned around two or three steps
from paradise, backtracking, blessed

to stumble again upon a watering hole
of the fierce wild cat & bull buffalo,
as snakes urged the tongue to speak

& shocked the eye into vivid color,
shades of green & gold in the grass,
bands of black & red promised survival

& just where darkness clouded blue
light has broken into rainbow, a covenant
of here & now, where an aftermath

proves tomorrow is on the horizon.
But look now at this icy stone-age
on the brink of becoming all water.

First, that taut medieval crossbow
still grabs my attention, & a catapult
made to hurtle stones & bloody

diseased gore across abyssal moats
& up over tall, stout fortress walls
at such a high, magnanimous hour,

we lament destinies scribed on sand
by the sea's unforgiving agitation
forged in a wind's lonely probe.

We lament blame plaguing us
as a fever sweeps over the seven
continents & we splash blood

of bull or lamb in the thresholds
of every doorway, where no gold
or crossbow can rescue us now.

We dig spades into muddy soil
to turn wormy earth before salvation
planted as medicinal gardens.

But sometimes it feels the past
held more living light than today.
How did ancients know to curb

those lucky ones from the dying
& dead, to sprinkle down quicklime
along the forbidden, winding paths,

to bury the tatters & burn the rats?
Now, please don't go quoting me
as today's refrain. That was 1347.

But still, have we forgotten all
we once knew? In these blessed days
of virtual minds spreading rumors

through cybersphere at near light-
speed, these zeros & ones can't break
a sweat. Learning once meant digging

your bare hands into silt & pulp
'til touch becomes another kind of sight.
Even a caveman knew how to hold

in focus four charcoal timber wolves
loping toward those two red horses
painted on the stony slanted ceiling,

telling us time flows where the brain
goes, as sunlight strikes the darkness,
before dreams become our masters.

Is this me sitting beside the boatmen
who sail to distant lands, far from love,
searching for aromatic herbs & spices?

Cinnamon & cardamom on the lips,
& raw cacao, food of the gods, harvested
from Theobroma trees, could cure me

of this troubled memory I can't seem
to shake. I keep moving the mind back
to first touch, & further to the music

of water in the womb where darkness
was my first comfort & I knew this
safety before it delivered me into the light.

In a time like this, on a night like this,
it's good to be in Papua New Guinea,
watching rainforest birds & orchids

coloring each day a hundred hues.
Birds-of-paradise take the heart
& mind for a run, & here I am.

I hear pounding feet of twelve men
chasing another group with spears
over to a wide circle of green grass

& here's the simple truth of submission,
whether a tribe bows in the brush,
whether plea or offering is enough to cast

spears down in a truce or else blood
must be shed to right whatever false step
has conjured these headhunters here.

I don't know, but tonight as the gods
would have it the pink moon rises
in Libra, scales balancing on a fulcrum.

I was asking why haven't I seen snakes
when I saw men rise from a mud hole,
smooth pale clay drying on their skin—

then a ritual of other warriors retreating
into the forest. Sloths in strangler figs
moved the day along. My feet said,

Run, but I didn't dare. I knew this
was still the land of the cassowary,
death adder, & roadside bandits.

But to stand & witness what makes us
afraid, no, I can't take any praise
for god-given lust of the eye, true

nature of being human, though we
onlookers may be condemned or blessed
to gaze long enough to see clearly,

unable to unsee or forget & not turn
to stone. Yes, grace or fortune led me
through mud with my head intact.

My eyes linger on the circle of grass,
& the interpreter says, Payback time.
Somebody's uncle was killed by a car.

At one time there would be blood
on that big circle, but not these days.
See the money tied to the spear-tips?

They must hand it over to the dead
uncle's clan, & now those receiving
give back half of the money. See?

Here, the old world & new collide.
No human sacrifice or Tasmanian wolf
slaughtered with his teeth crowned

in gold foil. Even in the forest, green-
backs pay a murder or quiet a godhead
& bloodthirsty clan of followers.

Yet deep in this land below the sunset
I can step into a clearing & look north
toward a peak silhouetting on Bird's Head.

Love, now please don't tell me the gods
hide in a broken field, munching on
fallen fruit, their feet in barren clay.

Let me show how it hurts, expanding
& tightening every throbbing muscle
till a worm drops from each romantic

eye, & plain whole true vision returns
as a lighthouse appears on the shore,
& a new dream ferries the body home.

Here & now we return to the dark news
of Hart Island where for fifty cents an hour
inmates from Rikers are digging trenches

in a potter's field three pine coffins deep
for nameless unclaimed dead somewhere
not too far from barracks where bare-knuckle

boxing once drew thousands to witness blood
shed on the same grounds confederate soldiers
were held prisoner & buried in common graves.

But even then, just a good holler away, boys
& girls from tenement flats lived to skip
frayed rope whipping against cobblestones

to tie the century together. The memory
of hunger lived in a world of young faces,
& a hard-working drunk's brash soliloquy

wounded the early evening sky. A non-stop
whine of machines pooled underneath
it all, stealing rhythm from the island.

Not so different now, across the Sound,
New Yorkers ride a storm in the heart
from Jackson Heights to Coney Island,

Harlem to the Rockaways, an underground
rhythm of trains a steady heartbeat
against immense silence where grief resides

'til a seven o'clock shift change, a chorus
of unbroken voices carries in a wave
of gratitude where no malady breaches us.

As doors of the Gilded Age fly open
one might still hear Walt Whitman
joking with counter-jumpers at Pfaff,

a lager saloon, taking notes for Calamus,
as Lower Eastside poor & robber barons
crossed paths, one hardly seeing the other,

but there was some great holler in a soul
wandering over to the foggy waterfront,
singing a dying language up to the sky.

Yes, on days like this time collapses
on itself & the world comes rushing in.
It's harder to see the streets so barren

without a hustle-bustle in the mind.
The way a coyote or band of racoons
might wander out of Central Park

up Fifth Avenue & climb the MET steps.
From the window, I watch newspaper
blow in the high winds barreling through.

Even if I count the streets out of bedlam
& know midnight winds howling down
cold-water flats, mouthing names for the

calamity—consumption, tuberculosis, or TB—
I also know the poor will inherit the hardest
blows. The ice, sleet, & snow, plot together

to ransack flimsy doors & cracked windows,
prying off shingles & spitting nails on the
ground, hammering the poor to their knees.

But the world now built is not the one man
inherited. I mean, factory smog & filth
yellow the horizon to reveal a broken skyline

where birds reckon into the wrong direction.
There's not a prayer that can undo the scythes
taking down the forests, or the fires burning

where bandicoots & kangaroos disappear
in billowing smoke, or how bats fly
into a market & unleash nature's wrath.

Look, I am hurting to go back to 1544.
When the Portuguese struck the heart
of Africa & prodded souls on schooners

down in the midnight hold for weeks
across the Atlantic, to a New World,
where oldest greed swallowed its own

barbed tail, & centuries later we are
here to question & leech the past,
speaking bluesy elegies to the future.

Even in dreams I cannot guard the gate
of no return, or turn over tables
where flesh & blood can be bought & sold.

No, a sacrificial lamb cannot pay dues.
No human, bull, or pig's blood blessing
a doorjamb can avenge ancestral labor.

Let's let dust be dust & seeds sewn
with blame bloom now into cantaloupe,
melons, & a field of wild berries.

Of course, there is always an outlier—
a black man such as Martin Alonso
Pinzon who captained the Pinta

in 1492, holding two or three worlds
inside himself—always a half-merciless
potion or cure told in a secret tongue,

saying what wild herb, earthen root,
fat bug or flower tincture steeped
into a brew to raise the near dead.

Ah, now, I know a drink or two
to wake a shade, a pinch of mugwort
& dash of horehound left in moonlight

if you're not afraid of seeing your own
reversal. Don't worry, love, there's nothing
in the world of mirrors that is not you

looking back. A sip of this or that reveals
undying darkness we all keep hidden,
but hocus pocus can leave one bitter.

Yes, we try to bloodhound a thousand
escapes, & outfox all known & unknown
maladies, to outrun fear itself, flexing muscles—

especially those cool hip young-bloods
& sheilas clutching death's-head pipes,
vaping sad flavors & aping moonshine.

We old ones, of course, spend last days
at bedroom, kitchen, or basement windows,
or busy ourselves fingering precious papers.

We know there's no way around fate's
finale, but, look, there's work to do
with what little time we might have left.

Somnambulists partying in their sleep
have caught themselves in a trap set
in one life or another. I know better.

There's a garden in mind & I must weed it
at dawn. See the fruit still growing there—
one late summer midnight, I'll eat it.

Well, this European woman saw
a tall Yoruba woman in the village
prick her son's thigh with an ivory

needle, & administer a pinpoint
of pox. The boy grew ill for three
days, but didn't possess a fever

or wall his eyes. Next day he rose
with two brown mourning doves,
asking, Mama, do I have a cane flute?

See he became the tune in him
& walked out into the village
calling the destiny names of ones

who did not rise that morning—
asking, *Has anyone seen Dada?*
Has anyone seen Joda? He blows

his flute to the hilltop, a prayer
to Oya, his breath a resurrection
or Atunwa song for those taken.

Now & then, let's say, a human
mind gloms with time, & grows
natural as a baobab beside a river

as a breeze shimmies green leaves,
& one may find himself anywhere
in this world, flying down overnight

through ages like a red hummingbird
across an angry sea, & an all-night
piano steals a mind in the Big Apple

riffing a phrase that works like a ruby-
throated birdcall against gridlock traffic
jamming up the noggin-box, a big moon

filling the skyline & everything wells up.
Yeah, I can hear Ellis clear through
a locked-down night sky where no smog

can hush pulse, syncopation, breath,
where we dwell on those days of the Village
Vanguard, or long ago in Snug Harbor.

I never left those Sunday afternoons
when Ellis's trio or quartet cooked on
the corner of Frenchman, celebrating

prophets long gone & not yet born.
Jason was nine, eyeing every move,
as his Daddy pulled it all together,

troubling the ivories. Last week, his
trembling left hand tricked the keys,
& then he crossed that wide river.

But we channel him back here
with a touch of "Mood Indigo"
on this upright, tuned by a blind man

who blesses the keys like a crow
calling in the hour between fate
& dawn. Yeah, we can follow

the song like the wide river running
between these states, like the devil
running from town to town, 'til we all

are on our lame & humble way. Mercy,
be with you. I may not be solely invincible
as Detective Baptiste, but I shall find hope.

Even in life's multiple disguises & blurry
pronouns, whoever we truly are, I am
three or four steps from your dominion.

Okay, forget the hummingbirds. I can't
stop thinking about those grasshoppers
floating in sea clouds to African rivers.

Yeah, I've only ever seen seventeen-year
cicadas emerging from their long tunnel lives
as nymphs, in total blindness, stumbling

drunks as they climb the weeping elm
into a resurrection, casting off the husk,
& awakening in a second body, ringing

cacophony of pure desire. But, no, hunger
of grasshoppers must arrive as devils,
ready to devour the world into dust.

Locust & plague? Indeed, I need an oud
& a hand-drum to master lamentation.
Run riffs down a spine, up a bittersweet

valley of trial & tribulation, & in no time
I am turning pages of Persian Pictures,
lost in Tehran, as the cholera scare

drives us toward the Caspian Sea,
on a road running northward where
cartloads of fruit fester in holy light.

For the Pandemics— Say What?

STEPHANIE STRICKLAND

STAR BLACK

STEPHANIE STRICKLAND's 10 books of poetry include *How the Universe Is Made: Poems New & Selected* (2019) and *Ringing the Changes* (2020), a code-generated project for print based on the ancient art of tower bell-ringing. Other books include *Dragon Logic* and *The Red Virgin: A Poem of Simone Weil.* She has published 12 collaborative digital poems, most recently *Liberty Ring!* (2020), a companion piece to *Ringing the Changes; House of Trust*, a generative poem in praise of free public libraries; and *Hours of the Night*, an MP4 PowerPoint poem probing age and sleep. Her work across print and multiple media is being collected by the David M. Rubenstein Rare Book and Manuscript Library at Duke University.

Time-Capsule Contents

1. Sermon: *What Will Be Left?*

Weather, certainly. Even
the ticking earth must thaw. Genetic law

will prove to be present, each still-born defect
confirmation. Murmurous

why-lords, why this generation? This destruction
of our marrow. More than all

these, memory of Promise, her chrysalis
jeans, her eyes extraordinarily

bright, shadowed with
mascara: Honey,

as she was,
in heat, in bloom, in slow

motion, left, locked
in the projector.

2. Transcription of Outtakes from Pre-trial Deposition

I don't think flu
should be our *whole* answer.
Let's go over it, again.

Be more specific, if you can.
This record has to hold
up, for generations. We do know,

Colonel, you've been ill.
And you say, you were misled,
or did you say, unnerved,

by a woman selling apples
who tried to stop you
on your way to work.

You ordered, *Two* if by land,
you chose, *North* Dakota,
you swore, If your *right* hand

offend you— Is this
the statement, Sir, you wish
to give the court?

3. Journal Entry

In the shelter, I doze.
I remember
Indian October. An aquarium of birchleaves

flowing around us
slowly,
like nectar. Home loaves.

Dark oven. Syrup
on our fingers. Chrysanthemums
heavy, in the sugarbowl

of summer.

Jus Suum: What Can Never Be Taken

Josiah Willard Gibbs, 1790-1861

... that the *question*
can be tolerated—whether they be

freemen—for
a single moment, Gibbs said

(Josiah Willard the Elder, Professor at Yale
of sacred books). *Language*

is a cast of the human mind
Gibbs Elder said, visiting the jail

in 1839, to give theirs back
to them, on "our" soil: transcribing

sounds, for words
for numbers, told to him

from behind their bars
when he held up his fingers: 1, 2, ... 5, ... 10;

then traveling to New York, by stagecoach,
ship, to the port, to seek—and find,

on a British brig, someone who spoke
Mendi *and* English,

that African men, Black mutineers,
might claim their right—should they

have had to? Inalienable—
in an American court,

convened in Connecticut, *New Haven,*
where the slaveship was tied up.

Our courts,
he said. The shame

to our courts, that the question could be tolerated
(whether

they be freemen—regaining their freedom—
or criminals, or property)

for a single

moment.

Burning Briar Scanning Tunnel

there is a zombie at the wheel
who finds acceptable all risk

(his flesh looks like mine)

a crinkle monkey in the swamp
mind tricky and brisk

(his moves feel like mine)

headless mannequin draped
white print snakeskin dress

(pale fakery filling me with dread)

a boneless man used up
by apparatchik juggernaut

(scrivener like me)

the one who hoped to poach
cockroach strategy adrift

(like me time-amnesic overreaching)

cord-cut all   beyond the call
to heal or heel   *fold   molt*

(wormhole crush crash course)

Black \ White

meter-..... made ..... screaming ..... *wah wah* ..... brass
      mutes ..... gag
swallow ..... gel-cling flame

vet cemetery in the Wasatch ... chestnuts ... flags
      brick
                 unutterable softness ... low
                     down ... wall
          climb in ... climb over ... quiet

                split \ \ \ *spilt* / / / *silt*
                domino / /
           \ \ \ \\ *drama* / / / /

disappeared ..... trousers afloat ..... float
         in the moonlight ..... button black a shadow
            drowned and soaking
                  white in the moonlight ..... haunt
     haint ..... zomboid ..... flow of clothes

in the twofold ... torn ... fold ... tangled ... river-
               entangled
pole ... pier

Virus

varieties of ecocide : does it matter
text 30001

viral vs. nuclear warheads :
answers at 10

we hear from gamers math professor
simulators those in actual rehearsal

involuntary
immersion in the real : a pharmal

target each blockbuster drug
to reach each until

it goes off-patent
factoid : leeches make shocking comeback

Body of Twisted Tangled Surfaces

beyond connectivity
beyond skeletal   interim
bendable
                body
                        body heap

proper harnesses and edges
        molded stapled suctioned
        no

rupture restively re-captured   X-
                plodes in
        side the
                        /mine

Hum

Stormer torches swing satellite protocol
trauma unit Bellevue stun
data Taser spew corrupted "that's all folks!" Fox [Ch. 5, 23, 91, . . .]

    —no more here than a squall racing
    the Sound
    shadowing the chop

belfry's balcony pagoda Yoda game
launch Fantasia sugar hit
keeping dogfight vision alive-like

    ironbanded famine flyswept eyes
    residual genedump scrip
    Reaper standing

nor raptor heaven neither un-ground-zoo-zeroed-zooming-in
op nor ozone-
wind-eaten harp nor treed panther porn

    killer / willing survivor re-brand blood
    bald men-in-black scorched
    commando titanium

women [. . . . .] black-sheet-wrapped grief-prone rocking
nor gazebo neither skybox
nor dell nor rill nor minaret nor fountain

Constant Quiet

constant quiet
    intercostal
        intercoastal green & silver
        muscled gillflesh slipping into
    opens out of
constant quiet

constant quiet
    Mississippi
        overflowing built a levee
        longer higher than the Great
    Wall of China
constant quiet

constant quiet
    building building
        horse paunch pistol man
        long back cropper convict
    steel muscled
constant quiet

constant quiet
    longer higher
        than the Great Wall of China
        Egypt Mississippi hunger
    flogged
constant quiet

constant quiet
      storm of air
            ocean storms
          River rising
     field gone train gone man gone
constant quiet

constant quiet
      who can open
          who can
        hold it
     constant
quiet

Fourth Fate • Spin-Steer

Musician

aerial fingering of theremins
fin rhythm tidings folding in all that
follows in the Cold World Order   all
paths are taken
              —mild acts of restoration
interfering diffract : Faith Ringgold's French
Collection Judith Gleason in mufti *I am
a witch* Bob Marley *no cry* Mark Twain
his raft Audre Lorde at a Barnard
Conference slaps timidity in the face
ark voice dragging by inches the old
reluctant white woman forward—
              Simone Weil : our pact
                              mind-&-world
must be re-struck

One Sentence To Save in a Cataclysm

Belief

in

the existence of other human

beings *as*   *such*

is

love

Simone Weil, *Gravity and Grace*

all things are made of atoms—particles that move   in perpetual
motion, attracting each other   when they are
a little   distance apart
but
repelling↔if↔squeezed↔into↔one↔another

The Feynman Lectures on Physics, Vol. 1, Ch. 1

the fairies' midwif' and she comes

. .. .

drawne with a teeme of little atomies

Romeo & Juliet, Queene Mab

at small scales a sugar space
&
    none   *no* time
        at
            all

Carlo Rovelli, *Reality Is Not What It Seems*

The Present Now

MARY JO BANG

MATT VALENTINE

MARY JO BANG is the author of eight books of poems—including *A Doll for Throwing, Louise in Love, The Bride of E, The Last Two Seconds*, and *Elegy*, which received the National Book Critics Circle Award—and a translation of Dante's *Inferno*, illustrated by Henrik Drescher. She's been the recipient of a Hodder Fellowship, a Guggenheim Fellowship, and a Berlin Prize Fellowship. She teaches creative writing at Washington University in St. Louis.

Today, worked on the notes for Purgatory XIX.

Today, worked on revisions to Purgatory XIX and notes for
Purgatory XX.

Today I thought, when this is finally over—

Today, did twenty-two notes and revisions to Purgatory XXXII.

Today I thought—as long as I don't die.

Today, did the notes to Purgatory XX, revised Purgatory XXI.

Today I had that fantasy hungry people have: that there will be
enough.

Today, did one note for Purgatory XXI and small revisions to
Purgatory XXII.

Today I thought, I feel even more tired than usual.

Today, revised Purgatory XXII, did three notes.

Today X emailed that she's washing her hands like a murderer.
Yes, Lady X, Act V, scene i.

Today X came in the evening and we talked about how crazy it is
that anyone can still be taken in by the people in power. And,
of course, about the virus.

Today, did the notes to Purgatory XXI, did revisions to
Purgatory XXI and XXII.

Today, there are too few test kits so not enough testing.

Today, all incoming travel from Europe has been stopped except
for US citizens.

Today, went to Dr. X early so I would be the first person to use
the room after the weekend. Still, I wore a mask.

Today I thought, life seems more or less normal except surely it
can't go on like this.

Today I thought, what about all the necessary parts of life, like
food production and processing and shipping.

Today, returned to the Purgatory XXII notes, which was a relief.

Today I explained to X that the idea is simply to slow the
development until we reach herd immunity, so as not to
overwhelm the hospitals and health-care workers.

Today I thought, I do feel the effects somehow, just being worn
down by the weight of it.

Today, did six Purgatory XXII notes. The effort is tedious and
    exhausting and slow-going.

Today I woke from a dream where X and I are still married
    and living in London. He says he doesn't want to be married
    anymore. I see that nothing I can say will change anything.
    In the dream, I rearranged the agency: he was leaving me
    instead of me leaving him. What was the same was the
    deep sadness and sense that nothing could be done, that
    something was over.

Today I thought, time has totally stopped. There is no
    foreseeable future and the present so overwhelms the past
    that it hardly exists.

Today I thought, I feel more tired, perhaps it's all the stress.

Today I felt anxious because when I got the mail, I pressed some
    packages to my chest.

Today the hospitals have no supplies and there are still no tests,
    or at best a few tests in a few places.

Today, less depressed but more anxious.

Today, reading X's *The Wendys*, I thought of how her work slices
    through the jugular, the wrist, and the femoral artery, i.e., it
    annihilates.

Today I meant to go back to the Purgatory notes but instead
    worked on translating X.

Today I tried to order groceries online but there were no
    delivery times.

Today I thought, someone in the building must be smoking
    these days. The smell of smoke goes on all day and makes me
    want to go outside or at least open a window but it's too cold
    for that.

Today, woke to the alarm at X. And then the sameness began.

Today I thought, the world is a teeming petri dish and I don't
    dare put myself in it.

Today there is a smell of stale smoke from morning to night and
    it is sickening.

Today X phoned. It cheered me considerably even though immediately after, I coughed up Keatsian blood.

Today, an email from X saying she was concerned that X might be very depressed and could I help him. I said I would suggest he and I Skype just to make sure he's okay but that there wasn't much I could do.

Today I emailed the neighbor upstairs about the strange smoke smell and she said she hadn't smelled anything and that she and her husband didn't smoke.

Today X texted to say the city of X had a first death, an X-year-old young woman with no known contacts.

Today I thought, as if anyone else in the world will care whether they read these translations.

Today the neighbor upstairs forwarded me a link about a condition called "Phantom Cigarette Smoke." It's associated with numerous medical conditions including respiratory illnesses.

Today I kept thinking of X. They texted last night with tragic news. I have to keep my mind from dwelling on it because that path always leads back to X's last hours and then the door to the world slams shut with such a deafening crash it knocks me backwards into the oubliette I lived in for so long.

Today, ordered groceries from X but they only had a few of the things I ordered.

Today, phone call from X saying Dr. X wanted to know how I was.

Today, email from X who says he's overwhelmed.

Today, finally got Dr. X's online platform to work on my phone but during the session, the screen began to pixelate and then the sound did too.

Today I talked to X, tried to convince him to stop obsessing about the virus news.

Today X phoned, he more or less said he thought I might die during the pandemic and that's why he was calling. That was cheery.

Today the day dissolved. Dr. X at noon. X phoned, she said there
was a complicated disaster at her office, which made me
think of Sartre's, Hell equals *les autres*.

Today the stock market plummeted: the egg has fallen off the wall.

Today I did the notes to Purgatory XXII, a few revisions to
Purgatory XXIII.

Today, texted with X. Emailed with X. To get a delivery slot for
groceries, I had to keep refreshing the page for hours.

Today, did revisions to Purgatory XXIII and a few notes.

Today, X emailed. She sent a photo of the two of us in
Switzerland looking at the eclipse! It was so long ago. X was
at rock bottom and I, on the other side of the world, could do
nothing about it.

Today I remembered when X and I saw the eclipse, there was
also the Mexican writer there who later died swimming in
the ocean: X. I just looked online and there he is, still. Born
1953, died 2001.

Today, finished revising Purgatory XXIII. Then revised
Purgatory XXIV and did five notes.

Today X sent me a CD, the Cowboy Junkies' *The Trinity Session*,
which made me think of X's death. Which made me think of
X's.

Today, finished the notes to Purgatory XXIII.

Today, tried to make a Zoom appointment with Dr. X to talk
about the phantom cigarette smell. A message machine said
the office was closed.

Today X phoned at 5:00 and we talked for a while. I said I
don't know whether I'll ever be able to go out into the world
without risking death.

Today Dr. X sent a message, saying the office was closed and
he was home with the coronavirus. He said he hoped to be
better by next Tuesday and would call then and if not, he
would ask one of his partners to get in touch.

Today, had a Skype session with Dr. X. When I talked about my fear of never leaving my apartment, she said not to think about the future, it's enough to deal with now.

Today, did six notes to Purgatory XXIV, a few revisions to Purgatory III.

Today, texted with X who says he might have the virus. He's going to try to get tested tomorrow.

Today, did more revisions to Purgatory II and did one note to Purgatory XXIV.

Today, worked on the notes to Purgatory XXIV. I only got nine done. There are ten more.

Today, X phoned. Email from X.

Today, finished the notes for Purgatory XXIV and began revising Purgatory XXV.

Today, phoned X. Email from X. She sounds well. To have that kind of tenaciously positive personality.

Today I ordered groceries. I should have ordered more but I had to move quickly or risk losing the rare chance.

Today, did revisions to Purgatory XXV, began working on notes for Purgatory XXV, did a few revisions to Purgatory XXVI.

Today I put the ladder on the dining room table and climbed up to remove the heavy glass shade and replace the burned-out bulbs. Then, poised at the top of the ladder—where the weight of the glass felt menacing—I put the shade back on.

Today, email from Dr. X's office, he's still not well enough to do teleconferencing. The scheduler offered to have me talk to another doctor in the practice. How long might it be before he's well?

Today called X and we talked for an hour. She said she thought it was wrong of Emily Hale to allow the Eliot letters to be read. What did I think? I said what I always say in these cases, the dead don't suffer. I hope I'm right about that.

Today, finished the notes for Purgatory XXV, did a few notes for Purgatory XXVI.

Today X brought by some items from the store. Cakes!

Today the trees were so strikingly beautiful from the window, I
wanted to be closer to them.

Today, all day on revisions to Purgatory XXVI. A few small notes.

Today, Skyped with Dr. X. I talked about death. When will that
be? Tomorrow or years from now. Hopefully not until after
Purgatorio is finished and in print. And the X translation.

Today I let time slip out of its cage and disappear in that way it
does where it leaves no trace.

Today I felt slightly short of breath, more tired than I have a
reason to be, generally not-well.

Today X sent back Purgatory II. I realized I should have told him
what I was doing with the angel that brings the penitents to
shore, trying to make the pronoun gender-neutral by using
they. He was confused by that and wrongly thought that I had
misunderstood and thought there were multiple angels on
board.

Today, long phone call with X. Mainly comparing notes about
how one reduces their risks.

Today, spent all day on notes to Purgatory XXVI.

Today, a note from Dr. X's office through the portal, he's still out
sick with the virus, another doctor will phone tomorrow.

Today, finished the Purgatory XXVI notes, although I got lost for
hours researching one of them.

Today had the teleconference with Dr. W. He suggested X and if
that didn't work, X.

Today finished revisions to Purgatory XXVII. Began to look at
Purgatory XXVIII.

Today I began to think the X is actually helping. But who
knows—so much is in one's head: Kafka's crawl space in
which something alive is always burrowing.

Today, did a few small revisions and eleven notes to Purgatory
XXVII.

Today, email to X. Writing about where I was with the
revisions and the beauty and sadness of Virgil's upcoming
disappearance, my eyes filled with tears. As Dante's will when

he realizes Virgil's gone. Such exquisite pain. As ED says,
"Parting is all we know of Heaven, and all we need of Hell."
Today, it seems impossible that the country is being run by
someone so craven.
Today I thought, Dante is right, greed is the worse sin.
Today I woke from a dream where I'm going on a trip with X.
At the airport, I realize I forgot my suitcase. Then I realize I
forgot my passport. When we land, X and I go to a restaurant
and as we're walking out, I lose sight of him. I go to phone
him and realize I've lost my phone. So, all is lost: suitcase,
passport, X, and phone.
Today, revisions to Purgatory XXVII.
Today I solved the X problem in Purgatory II, did two notes to
Purgatory XXVII.
Today X and I had a FaceTime visit from 6 to 8. It was sweet, I
put on music, as if it were a real visit.
Today, wrote a note for Purgatory XXVII.
Today, an email from X, inviting me to write poems for a small
anthology. I feel unable to say no to such a kind ask but I also
wonder whether I could write anything at this point, when
I'm so immersed in the *Purgatorio*.
Today, texted with X, a bit with X. And then with X. Today is my
half-birthday. It feels as if hardly anything happened before X
arrived. And nothing but sorrow since he left.
Today, finished the notes to Purgatory XXVII, although I'm
stuck on the last line.
Today, woke from a dream where I'm in a car with X, we've been
trying to decide where we will live together and he says that
he has to tell me something: he's bought a condo in Chicago
and he's decided to work there. I try to get him to clarify
but he keeps evading my questions. The dream echoes the
unpleasant conversation with X, his evasiveness, my feeling
of: Just fucking tell the truth.
Today, an email from X. Skype session with Dr. X. The painful
memories of X lying. The continued disquiet.

Today, email to X to say yes to the anthology. Opened the mail
   that was piling up on the long bench, left there partly for
   decontamination, partly out of disinterest.
Today, went over Purgatory XXVII and the notes. Began revising
   Purgatory XXVIII.
Today, woke from a dream where I was at a conference
   and Bob Dylan was there. The first night we had a brief
   pleasant conversation at dinner but the next day, he was
   always surrounded by a group of male fiction writers and
   I could see, I was too insignificant to get to have a second
   conversation with him.
Today texted with X. We are both feeling hopeless about the
   world. I have to remind myself I do get work done, however
   slowly these days.
Today, worked on revisions to Purgatory XXVIII and finally
   finished them.
Today X phoned. He says this weekend is supposed to be the
   peak of the infections.
Today, phone call from X. Revisions to Purgatory XXVIII and a
   few notes.
Today, email to X, text with X and X. In the background, the
   Cowboy Junkies mixed with St. Vincent and Dylan.
Today I thought, how odd I'm here in the Midwest, whether
   I want to be or not. A pure product of this place and now
   I've lived in St. Louis longer than anywhere else: Chicago,
   Philadelphia, London, New York City, with stays in Berlin and
   Bellagio and Liguria, and Lavigny. Now locked in by the virus.
Today I thought, sometimes it feels as if a concrete slab has
   toppled from above onto my chest and then I think, be
   patient, this will end.
Today I thought, "... thóughts agaínst thoughts ín groans grínd."
Today I woke tired and thought how tired I am of the sameness.
   Worked on notes for Purgatory XXVIII.
Today I thought, life is that bottomless basket of shirt sleeves

that had to be set into shirt-fronts that day in 1972 when I
worked at a garment factory. Just when I thought I was near
the finish line, someone brought a new basket.

Today, more revisions to Purgatory XXVIII and began revisions
to Purgatory XXIX.

Today, texted with X. He's exhausting himself. I worry for him.

Today, texted with X. Email with X about the editorial question.

Today, more revisions to Purgatory XXIX and the first two
notes. Got lost looking up Guido Cavalcanti poems and
reading about those.

Today, felt more rested but still having a hard time
concentrating. Emails to X. Email from X, asking how I am.
One from X, also asking how I am.

Today, text from X saying he and X talked for a long time on the
phone today about how important my teaching was to them.
That nearly broke my heart, the sweetness of it.

Today, email from X, who's going to be furloughed for three
months beginning Friday.

Today, worked on the intro note for the X poems and emailed it.
That took two hours, which is ridiculous since it was only a
few sentences.

Today, raining, varying shades of gray. Emmy Lou Harris is
warbling in the other room, "What you lost when you left
this world," making my eyes fill with tears. I think the X
experience has destabilized me. I really haven't gotten much
work done since, just what has to be done.

Today, went over Purgatory XXVIII and made tiny changes.

Today, woke from a dream where I have to drive a city bus. I
think, the seat is too high, my feet won't touch the pedals, so I
pull myself up using the hang bar and stand behind the seat.
But then I think, how is this going to help?

Today, the heartrending obits. The talent, the years spent
becoming, and now wiped out. How did they get the disease?
Didn't they know to not see anyone?

Today I thought, I can't die yet, not until *Purgatorio* is finished.
Then fine, I'll close my eyes and invite the angel of oblivion to
push my head under the waters of Lethe and hold it there.

Today, worked on revisions to Purgatory XXIX all day.

Today, tears several times. I don't know what has thrown me
into this ocean of sorrow. Perhaps watching all the suffering
that is so much worse than mine. And the idiocy, the
hatefulness, the intransigence that keeps it all in place.

Today, finished the notes to Purgatory XXIX.

Today, email from X yesterday saying he too had been thinking
of me. X brought me cake and left it on the doormat. Today
was much better than yesterday.

Today, finished the notes to Purgatory XXIX yet *again*. A few
notes to Purgatory XXVIII.

Today the day is sunny and cake for lunch. I tried to trim my
bangs but the scissors are so dull, I didn't achieve much.

Today, Zoomed this evening with X and X. It was a rather perfect
evening and cheered me. Told them the X story.

Today, worked all day on notes to Purgatory XXVIII. Only two
left to do. There were so many. Also did more research about
X and changed that note in Purgatory II. And did research for
the note in Purgatory XXXIII.

Today, I texted X to see how she was. The exchange was brief. I
always thought we would be friends forever but we aren't now
and won't ever be again. That is a source of sadness but it was
a myth that we could have stayed friends. I did love her. Once.

Today, finished the notes to Purgatory XXVIII. Set up the notes
to Purgatory XXIX and did maybe fifteen.

Today, woke from a dream about X. As usual, complications
ensued. My dreams somehow want to mirror my life back to
me, as if I need confirmation of my powerlessness.

Today, X texted back. What I miss so much about her is her
humor. Text from X, we're going to have a Zoom night
sometime this week.

Today, email from X to say that X is not doing well. How I wish
I could help but I know there is no helping him. Text from X.
There too, I wish I could do something and there is nothing
that can be done. Pain will be. And inside my own head, the
circus of sorrow spins and spins, day after day.

Today my O2 level is down, I think because I'm so inactive. I
keep waiting for a day warm enough to go outside but it's
either too cool or raining. X phoned. Worked on notes to
Purgatory XXIX.

Today there was another text from X. Maybe this is where it
should stop. Otherwise, there will be that knife that causes
such exquisite pain.

Today, texted with X, after which I ended up sobbing. X's death
brings back X's and there I am, back in a Beckett play saying I
can't/I will go on.

Today, worked on notes to Purgatory XXIX. I'm dead inside.

Today, talked to Dr. X. She said I should get in touch with Dr. X
about the X dose, that we should think of that as laying down
a layer of bedrock. Yes, I said. But have done nothing.

Today, X and I talked at 5 for an hour or so. That was nice. He
asked about X and we went back over that situation. I didn't
talk about the X situation. So many situations.

Today, worked on the notes to Purgatory XXIX. I keep reading
over Purgatory XXX. Since January, I've worked so steadily
and have had so much stress, so much isolation. And then
the coronavirus, and then X.

Today, worked on the notes to Purgatory XXIX, which I'd
thought were finished.

Today I thought, what drives me, besides the fear of dying
before the translation is finished. And then I thought, the
primitive mind that lives in fear is driving this car and has
since I was a very small child.

Today, a few revisions to Purgatory XXX.

Today X phoned. She says things are improving in Germany.

They are cautiously beginning to go outside and see
others.

Today, email from X saying X had died. She'd been ill so it might
be better to go now rather than endure more indignities
but it was sad to think of it. She was always so bright and
intelligent.

Today, a few small revisions to Purgatory XXX. I went to the
garage and found the car battery was dead.

Today, emails to X, to X, and to X. Sent X a revised list of
questions because I'd answered one of the questions I'd sent
earlier. Long phone conversation with X, the X story. Texting
with X. How I miss him. My eyes fill with tears as I write that.

Today, stayed up late last night so all day my mind has been in a
fog. A few emails: to X, who'd emailed to see how I am, and to
X.

Today it occurred to me, why not let the car just sit there since
I'm going nowhere for a while. Revisions to the poem I began
on Sunday.

Today, worked on the notes to Purgatory XXX but got nowhere:
the first note's confusion about X vs. Y kept me busy but
since the question can't be resolved, it was all wasted time.

Today, all day working on the notes to Purgatory XXIV. For no
apparent reason, I found myself crying. My idiotic Eliotic
whimpering at the world's end.

Today, I found reading the paper excruciating: the jobless rate,
pig farmers slaughtering their stock, one spending the entire
day shooting them individually, another sealing the barn and
pumping in carbon monoxide. Meanwhile children are going
hungry.

Today, states are opening back up and people are stupidly
crowding into bars and trying to hold concerts. I can't watch
this much longer. I don't know how people are managing.

Today X phoned. Did eight notes to Purgatory X.

Today, logged onto the Zoom memorial, which was quite moving.

It's been raining off and on all day, every time I've thought I would walk, it started up again. Now dark clouds are rolling in, which makes me not want to go out even though I promised myself I would today.

Today, finished Purgatory XXX. I read over Purgatory XXXI to see what needed revising.

Today, raining out. All day I've done nothing except for texting with X, who had a very ugly incident with X. I'm going to try to not work on notes or revisions tomorrow.

Today, did a few small revisions to Purgatory XXXI, especially the first two tercets. The notes weren't nearly as close to being finished as I thought. They're barely begun.

Today at some point, I convinced myself it was Sunday. That's how it goes now, no sense of days or weeks. A perpetual purgatorial now.

Today, I went out, which felt like a triumph of sorts since I can always find reasons not to go. It began to rain or I might have stayed out longer. Emailed X to see how she is. X emailed. Now the sun is out.

Today, I'm calmer than I've been for a while, for a week at least.

Today, all day on revisions to Purgatory XXXI, and just now, six notes. I should be able to finish the notes at least by the end of Thurs, if not before.

Today, email from X. She said she's been having visitors outside, at a distance of 6 feet. It made me wonder whether I might do something like that, outside, at a distance. Perhaps. After the *Purgatorio* manuscript is turned in. That idea is cheering.

Today I had an email from X giving me the pub date and production schedule. I just wrote to X to ask whether he would do the cover.

Today, finished Purgatory XXXI this evening. Only Purgatory XXXII left to do.

Today, answered emails to X, X, X, and X. Texted with X, X, and X. Skyped with Dr. X.

Today, the entire day setting up the notes for Purgatory XXXII,
   did a few of them. A few small revisions to the canto.

Today, all day on the notes to Purgatory XXXII. I need to read
   over the entire thing.

Today, I went back through emails to see when I began working
   on *Purgatorio*. It was 2012, even before *Inferno* was out. I got
   stuck after Purgatory III because I couldn't make myself do
   the notes. And then it wasn't until 2014 that I began again. So,
   it's been eight years, not seven as I'd been thinking. Add that
   to the seven for *Inferno* and it's fifteen years.

Today, feeling dull and deadheaded. I just realized I wouldn't
   have enough time to translate *Paradiso*, even if I wanted to.

Today, I'm feeling more and more apart from the world. It feels
   like *Purgatorio* is too small a thing, the river of sorrow has so
   much in it.

Today, worked on correcting the manuscript and notes. I only
   finished the first three cantos.

Today, worked on Purgatory VI. The corrections are taking so long.

Today, from morning until now and I've only revised Purgatory
   VII. There are not enough days left to spend this much time
   on each canto.

Today, did the notes and a few more revisions to Purgatory VIII,
   and revisions and notes to Purgatory IX. This is not going
   fast enough.

Today, texted a bit with X, who helped me solve a word choice
   problem.

Today, the country over the weekend exploded in violence over
   yet another senseless murder of a Black man, George Floyd, by
   a white cop with a history of violence. How long can this go on?

Today, woke from a dream where X comes in and says X and
   then I'm with X, and later with X. So much activity and all
   while I'm supposed to be sleeping.

Today, finished notes and revisions to Purgatory XII and

Purgatory XIII and revisions and notes to Purgatory XIV.
Then finished revisions to Purgatory XVIII.

Today, the news is so grim. The problems are so entrenched, and
only keep worsening. I realized last night, Michael Brown's
death was six years ago. Six years and so many deaths since.

Today, only managed to do the notes for Purgatory XVIII and
revisions to Purgatory XIX.

Today, from outside, the intermittent flow of sirens. How to
bring about lasting change, I can't fathom how but there are
those who can.

Today, woke from a dream where X and I were in an elevator on
our way to our offices on the 21st floor of a high-rise building.
The elevator began to shake at one point and I thought, how
many stories will we have to walk up? But then the shaking
stopped.

Today, all day on revisions to Purgatory XXV. Just read through
Purgatory XXVI.

Today, woke foggy-headed at 9. Skyped with Dr. X today. I said I
felt depressed but the dead kind, not the sobbing kind.

Today, I had hemoptysis. It's always a shock. Worked all day on
the translator's note. Hopefully tomorrow I can return to
correcting the notes. X texted.

Today, the world outside continues to be one of protests.

Today, worn away by this work and by the world.

Today, corrected the notes for Purgatory XXXIII and Purgatory
XXXII. Revised Purgatory XXXI and Purgatory XXXII.
Sometimes it all blurs.

Today, stayed in bed this morning for an hour because of the
reluctance to begin the sameness.

Today, saw a sculpture called "X" online. I felt such intense
sadness looking it. It kept haunting me until I looked up the
artist. Yes, sadness: orphanage and alcohol and suicide at 47.

Today, worked on revisions to Purgatory XXVII. X sent the

anthology with my response to Auden's "Poetry Makes Nothing Happen."

Today, Zoomed at 5 with X, which felt like a lifeline. Texted with X. She goes up and down, she said. I said, yes, that is how grief is. I had a 30-minute FaceTime session with Dr. X. We're going to try X.

Today, worked on the notes all day and a few revisions. Spent way too much time on one tercet in Purgatory XXXIII. Went over the translator's note edits that X sent and made those changes and then talked to her and sent her the new version.

Today, an email from X. And one from X in response to an email from me saying I admired his collaboration with X on the X website.

Today, after midnight, sent everything to X—then once I was in bed, after 2 and unable to sleep, I realized I hadn't numbered the pages, so today I sent everything again as one numbered document. So, it's more or less finished. I still have to do the sources. I printed it all out today.

Today, emailed X to thank him for the brilliant "Quotation" he sent weeks ago. Every so often, I think about the fact that soon X will be due. Then I think, that's X days away, it's not possible! And then I keep doing whatever I have to do at the moment.

Today, texted with X. Wrote a poem, "The Problem of the Present."

Today, Skyped with X. Talked about how the idea of never being able to travel again or see people in person makes me wonder whether a life like that would be worth going on with.

Today, a text and phone call from X. Then AAA came to start the car, which needed a new battery after all this time sitting. Email from X. Texted with X.

Today, woke in the night in a state of panic. Slept again and woke feeling completely at sea.

Today, Dr. X said a vaccine was probably two years away, that

that is what those in his field are thinking. He said I could walk in the park if I avoided people but until there's a vaccine, I shouldn't travel.

Today, emailed X the essay. Email to X about the crack in the pipe, asking whether it has in fact worsened since January?

Today I thought about Barthes and wondered, who living today would dare say the author is dead when we are trying so hard to just be.

Today, texted with X. My mood is Wordsworthian: The world is too much. Too much with me.

The Life After

SHANE MCCRAE

SHANE MCCRAE is the author of *In the Language of My Captor*, which was a finalist for the National Book Award, the Los Angeles Times Book Prize, and the William Carlos Williams Award; *The Animal Too Big to Kill*, winner of the 2014 Lexi Rudnitsky / Editor's Choice Award; *Forgiveness Forgiveness*; *Blood*; and *Mule*. He is the recipient of a Whiting Writers' Award and a National Endowment for the Arts Fellowship. He teaches at Columbia University and lives in New York City.

with the draining of summer, shadows bleed and spread

—Geoffrey Hill

I Hear the Wild Birds Singing Tangled Roads

It's eight o'clock   in the morning I have opened
A window in Manhattan twice as tall
As it is wide window   on the fourth floor
　　In our the sticker on the door

A sticker like the sticker on the door
Of a hotel room I have opened a
Window in our   the sticker says it's fire-
　　Proof I have opened at the far

End of our fire-proof building in our fire-proof
Apartment at the back   that stretches from
The middle of the building to the back
　　Our building next to the big rock

So big you hadn't noticed it our daughter
Who next to me before had leaned not *out*
Not through the   screen but to the edge of the window
　　Leaned *to* the window even pointed

Not through   the screen but if I hadn't known she
Was pointing at the rock I might have thought she
Was pointing at the screen   and not the rock
　　But she was pointing at the rock

And when I told her when I said the thing she
Was pointing at was   a big rock she looked
At me like she was looking at a screen
　　Like she had stopped   to look at the thing

She was supposed to look through   I had hoped she
Would look through me to see the thing I told
Her was the world   the big   rock in it but
    How long   ago last week we stood

In front of the rock   and she said she had never
Seen it or she had seen it   but had thought
It was a road (the screen makes   grids on things
    Like land surveyors make)   so big

It's not a natural part of the world   it's eas-
ier to think a will like   hers the will
That made our building that   stands where it stands
    Because of it was   a hundred and

Twenty-four years ago developers
Who didn't want to   spend the money to
Blow up the rock it's   easier to think
    The will that makes the window makes

The rock   it's   nine twenty-six I have opened
A window I have stood   at the screen at the window
And only heard I hear   now only still
    Birds   their songs clashing now and full

Of no one walking where before   of the
Gone people who before   soaked up the singing
I hear the wild birds singing tangled roads
    I see the rock that was a road

Skating Again at Forty-Four

A kickflip first a kickflip   first because
It was the last trick I learned well enough
I wouldn't most of the time   fall doing one

At forty-four I tried a kickflip first
When I at forty-four again I set
A skateboard down again   and stood on it

Before I even   tried to ollie even
Though kickflips not the   freestyle kind the street
Kind always   start with ollies   like how human

Beings always start with being   fish a kickflip
Starts with an ollie   just a   leap with the board
Into the air   the skater snaps the tail

Of the board against the ground   and leaps   and drags
The skateboard up by sliding their the   foot
They didn't use to   snap the tail against

The ground the other foot their front foot sliding
It toward the nose of the board   dragging the board
Free from the ground   but then the skater breaks

The ollie kicks the   board and the board rotates
Once in the air   before the skater stops its
Rotation with their back foot guides the board down

I tried a kickflip first   because I felt
Confident with them last   before I quit
The last   time I quit skating   after I

Had quit a dozen times before   though quitting
Skating was less me   stopping doing some-
thing *that*   particular thing regular-

ly with my body more me   saying but to
Whom   to myself   to nobody me saying
I'm not a skater anymore as if

Instead I might have said *I'm not a living*
Being anymore and died   the day I quit I
Had driven to the skatepark   in the middle

Of the day   because the kids who usually
Would be there would it was   a weekday be
In school I went   when nobody would see me

A thirty   minute drive to the park   I set my
Board down   and right away I didn't want
To skate the   park was empty   and I only

Wanted to launch my board from the quarterpipes
Without me launch it   riderless as high
And far as it would go   and sometimes my

Board flipped before it landed on its wheels
And that would look like some invisible
Skater some ghost had   meant for it to flip

Some ghost   had flipped the board and rolled away
And sometimes my   board flipped and spun in ways
Nobody could have   meant or rolled away from

Before I drove back home I did one kickflip
On the flat in the empty park   to prove I could   to
Prove I was still the ghost of me   the last

Time I quit skating   I was thirty-nine
I had learned kickflips twenty years before
But mastered them nine years before   when I

Mastered them even   as I mastered them
I knew   skateboarding wouldn't   bear my fan-
tasies of my life anymore I was

Thirty I was   in law school I was learning
Quitting was in everything I learned
And stepping on a board again at for-

ty-four not   learning but just   trying to
Remember what I had most recently
Learned quitting was   I felt it now in

Remembering   I stood on the concrete slab on
My skateboard on the concrete slab behind my
Apartment in a city where there isn't

A city anymore   pretending to
Be somebody I couldn't be again
Again   at forty-four   I had become a

Virus in my own body   fighting it
To live in it   and still I crouched   and leaped and
Leaping I kicked   the board and the board spun

Into a void I felt a void appear in
My memory   and still I caught the board
With my back foot stopping   the spin and pulling

The board back   from the void my body pulled
It back my back foot knew   its place in the air
Before I knew I still knew how to kickflip

As if my body were   haunting my body
As if the ghost   whispered at last its message
My body to my body   and it stopped

The spinning that continued in my mind
Continued   for a second or two after
I stood on the board on the ground again my arms

Out like a gliding seagull's wings   my body
Wobbling like a seagull gliding in
Strong gusts of wind   and the wind says to the seagull

Where are you now   that I have changed without
Telling you I had changed where   are you now
Who once had thought you were at home in me

When Our Grandchildren Ask Us What America Was Like Before

We lived in giant   tin eagles we used rags
Wrapped around human bones as torches we were dogs
Each dog in its own bird   we didn't speak
To each other but   yes we could talk
Yes they could hear us yes   they didn't answer
Our questions   but they heard
Us we spoke light   to light the corners too   dark for the
    torches
Those shadows even light   from burning bones won't touch
    yes

A god's shadow   is cast inside
Its body   no they weren't gods
No   more like noises made   music by dancers
We made the shadows then   we searched
The shadows then we made new shadows when we danced
Again   we spoke around the torches no   we could-
n't hold them like you would we had   no hands
We held them burning in our teeth and smiled

Into the Shot

At the end of the world more world world never-ending
Non-human world   birds from the trees like pollen
And pollen from the flowers   yellow as canaries
Black pigeon on the arch

Above the bricked-up window   wearing yellow
I used to think I was competing   and the pigeons begged
Between my toes   and now I stand at the bricked-up window
Wearing my new black Berg-

man T-shirt   camera in my hand   and shout
And shout   and I can't shout the pigeon
Into the shot I want   in the shot
It's gliding from the arch   to the statue of a thin man stand-

ing on the back of a thin man   it's maybe
Ten feet   from the arch to the statue   and I catch
The pigeon just   before it lands   its wings un-
furled like the angel's its black claws   extended what's

The angel's name   to grip the head

The Second Death

Forgiven by the rainbow into life
Again the drowned climbed death   part of their faces
Now that before   had borne life only
The drowned climbed back   to the places

They had once occupied
Some to high temples some   to higher towers
From everywhere   they were they scanned   sleeplessly now
   the valley
For what they saw now after everywhere

Death everywhere   not only in the confused shadows
But in the thin sunlight now after   the first and smaller flood
Some scanned the distant blue-brown forests
For death some scanned   the slowly healing ground

For death   to burst or seep from the gaps between
The branchless trees that stood like furrows standing   from
The gaps   between the furrows where the youngest planted
Trees furiously some

Sat in their huts and peeled the faces
From the whittled sticks that had with the flood drifted
From countries   they couldn't imagine
Though sometimes they   saw their own faces on the whittled

Sticks   and always they   stabbed those sticks deeper
They left unmutilated the   few sticks that bore instead of faces
Animals they didn't recognize
Thick-muscled flame-tailed   beasts some thought were wolves
   some horses

Birds with long beaks   so sharp some of the drowned
Used them instead of knives   to cut
Their own contorted faces from the sticks   themselves
Feeling like gods then   as they cut   or not

Human at least   as far from human
As God was far from them when they cried from the water
For God's help   that was the first death
The second death is the life after

By the Oceans of Styx, We Knelt and Wept

KEN CHEN

KEN CHEN is the recipient of the Yale Younger Poets Award, the oldest annual literary award in America, for his book *Juvenilia*, which was selected by the poet Louise Glück. He served as the executive director of the Asian American Writers' Workshop from 2008 to May 2019. An NEA, NYFA, and Bread Loaf Fellow and National Book Award judge, Chen co-founded the cultural website *Arts & Letters Daily* and CultureStrike, a national arts organization dedicated to migrant justice. He has been quoted in NPR's *All Things Considered*, the *Wall Street Journal*, CNN, the *New Republic*, the *New Yorker*, and the *New York Times*. A graduate of Yale Law School, he successfully defended the asylum application of an undocumented Muslim high school student from Guinea detained by Homeland Security. He was a Cullman Fellow at the New York Public Library, where he worked on *Death Star*, a book about his traveling to the underworld and seeing there everything that has been destroyed by colonialism. He is represented by The Wylie Agency.

Each night I would read a little bit before going to sleep. The notion of visiting the underworld filled me with an anticipatory excitement and also dread. Over the months and years that would pass, I began to gain a basic fluency in the avenues and neighborhoods of death. And as I began to travel there more regularly, I found myself astonished by the thick stream of traffic heading toward mortality, the sheer numbers of the dead, the faces that I recognized. Carolyn Forché writes, "how secretly you died for years, on behalf of all who wished for themselves a private death"—the opposite of how so many people now exit life emanating a halo of smartphone transmissions and social media posts. How strange that the death of so many people has now become public when it should be private, or perhaps private when it should be public, when we should all know the havoc that the silent systems hide. I had not died, I was not one of these pilgrim-ghosts, but I tried to do what I could to note who they had been. We live in the time of martyrs and the living dead, the not-yet-dead who now countenance the apocalyptic politics of our time. Life pried from bodies, bodies deprived of souls, this dismembering and remembering available for everyone to witness. How has death grown overpublic? Everyone privy, every human allowed to abrase their souls upon each fresh death.

I. OVERTURE

How is it that everyone is dying lately?
All headlines transmuted into elegies,
Death the lupine drone slips free all fetters, eager
to dispense its love and we read the luminous inscription of names
on our handheld 5G gravestones, doomscrolling they call it
(swipe right: authoritarianism), the tablet an epitaph
that we the living bear. We shall go to greet the arrival

of new ghosts—and that is how we came to the mortal
    borderland
and saw so many faces we recognized, how we followed
the procession of new migrants toward hell.
Come let us greet each soul we pass.
Surely this is the least we can do, there have come so many
so many new ghosts that surely we must note them all.
Let us not be Whitman of the settlers saluting, O shout instead
the empire's obituaries read under sallow iPhone lamp.
Let us be we.
Each passing day, the waves of Styx break new ground, spilling
    out
national specters. Recite, recite, as we watch the former people
washing ashore. We dreamed we saw those beloved dead
whose names grew public past naming.
A man dozing by the Wendy's drive-thru, a woman slumbering
when her boyfriend hears men invading. Did you know
even dreaming has been criminalized?
The passionate mass of names grows each day, the weight
stronger than our finite incantations can levitate.
A nightclub bouncer howls for his mother, does he press his ear
to the ground to listen for her shadow's response?
No, another man pressed him
to the street, he famished him for air.
Recite over alerts and pressers,
past phone notifications and the wet noise of coughs!
Shout over the police who have prohibited even breathing.
We shall erect sad mythologies, let us pour
a postscript foundation, set frame for the astral mausoleum
of those who left owning only their names.
O how we shall outmason the monuments!
Lay down a concrete mixed from the ephemerality
of shouts, the chants we exhale so wondrously contagious,
that our infected flame shall dissolve

all statues and the very state.
And against the vast unliving quiet of the universe,
the force of our sighs unmoors the earth from its spindle,
the planet spools out its fraying thread of days,
arson of Amazon and Australia, Grenfell Tower
and Golden State, where they threw hoses at prisoners
and led them into the burning forest.
Borne through air comes plague and pestilential hornets, no too
    easy
to call apocalypse, too easy to blame God
and eschatology when something
even more predatory hunts us,
the fellow humans.

II. STORY OF THE DELUGE

We dreamt of water, element of reflection
and the unconscious, aerosol droplet, container ship.
We saw beside us ten houses swimming,
they flew across the surface of the flood,
and we saw a mother surfing her roof on this planet
careening its long curve through space. No. No, this never
happened. What we saw was people on their roofs beseeching
helicopter newscams for help, we saw the ocean painting
these poor people into the corner of the sky. Abdicate
the lyric urge, describe instead the mythopoetic absence.
We dreamed of New Orleans
where no wrathful God sent deluge, no God here at all,
only Louisiana levees weakened austere,
Memorial Medical Center crammed and also abandoned,
the patients euthanized against their wishes, even a Superdome
can become a camp for those who fled the water, no Noah,
no Ark, simply stark disinvestment, these divinatory images

foretelling our present, so ashamed of our failed nation
we hide our faces behind masks.
Never forget September 20!
Once cursed by Maria's winds, even the ground shivers
in fear of FEMA and colonial numbers
and after the earth calmed, after the people slept in tents
for weeks—what does it mean to be afraid
of your own home?—after someone found the warehouse,
packed with so much baby powder, bottled water wrapped in
    plastic,
portable stoves, propane tanks, this lair of state failure
and profane abundance, there came out the protestors,
can you blame them for bringing guillotines
to marches? We saw that they carried them supine
in the manner of pallbearers.

We dreamt of gluttonous water swallowing so many,
utter force slamming down Sri Lanka and Fukushima
and when the floods fall back, newly melted waves claim
their watermark. WAH WAH WAH they cry!
O how their eyes spill up sublime drops,
the wilting glaciers weep loud the tears of the world flood!
Sad penguins starve in winter heat, the Arctic balmier
than Brooklyn. WAH WAH Young flood pouring
forth corpse of glaciers.
We dreamed the world's corral forest blanched white
from the sweat of bathing tourists. We dreamed the reef left
its skeleton to gesture
toward the last living beasts of water.
We dreamed of the Mogaveera who long guarded the shore
where now bull trawlers scrape and light fishers lure
all spawning swimmers.
We dreamed of the fishermen of Conakry
who haul their scanty catch towards sellers

on the shore, scattering a second tide of silver fins
and bins of cheap plastic, these seamen
who have long tasted the savor
of drawing a fish and smoking it.
Now factory ships have hoisted half the fish
into the strange suffocations of the air—O abject rapture
    Devonian,
I had not known
you could sack the sea!
Famished men chew game once thought too gristly to eat,
bonobos, fruit bats, civets, beasts for the vector
now uprooted by the loggers.
Did you know they have erected the sky
in Amazonia? How the horizon must look perverse
to the Guajajara, those like Paulo Paulino who know
you can see the open air only
because the trees have left their specters.
Humans and other planetary beasts,
please summon your solidarity for forests, coral
and the piscine dead.

By the oceans of Styx, we knelt and wept.
Once a river, once a wet filament necromantic.
Now the mortal border fattens moist and inundates
and a newly poured ocean floods the earth.
Sublime floods prowling the deserts.
We came upon travelers who walked from dry lands south,
they said their names were Rosa and Óscar
and they held their daughter Valeria, not yet two,
while they walked the intersection of the Rio Grande and Styx.
Óscar carried Valeria across and swam back for Rosa.
This was when Valeria followed her father
into the river. What choice did he have?
He leapt into the waters

and the current tore them away, stronger
than his desperate strokes
and weaker than their embrace. Why
why do we possess a photograph of this?
The photograph too horrific to see.
Your eyes shun it instinctively.
We dream of Óscar in his black skullcap carrying Valeria
for she is still his baby. On his shoulders, she sings
and plays a toy guitar. Her songs spill over other waters
and drift where another mother
can faintly hear them.
We learn that her name had been Rehana.
Even as a child, she had feared the water.
Kleptomaniac ocean, so greedy to snatch
any desperate vessel, smothering those sailors propelling
toward capital's barricades. She plucks the armpit of her life vest,
a fake she now knows. They had overcrowded the vessel in life.
At least here Charon's rubber raft ferries only light cargo,
the weight of specters being only psychic. The skiff docks and
     she sees
her child on the shore. Walking on the balls of her feet,
she gently lifts her son,
who had been lying face down on Bodrum beach.
A child named Alan.
Obscene image, have you ever seen a stillness so profane
your eyes sting?
In this place, he stirs, he wakes.
What dark sentimentality.

III. RIVER OF NAMES

Imagine Styx drowning vowel Tower long ruined,
Babylon ziggurat by River eroded, tossing loose now
multilingual stones into flood-drift,

Styx and stones, brook and bones, words will never hurt me,
would neighbor heard me, world willow weep for me, form me,
Babel Ocean speaking superflux and syllables, speak we and
fluidity, spilling fluent spates of every tongue, flumes, and
streams, tributes spoken,, each tine splitting off divergent
tributaries,, humans floating the cosmos of epitaphs, _____
New York judge in the Hudson,, _____ of Talahassee who said
she could not strip the color from her skin, _____ carried down
the Schuylkill River Philadelphia, no, no, insufficient, such
insufficient surfeit does little more than name the lost, name
those surffering, sic, sick, names as embarrassing surplus, surf
plage, en plus, pluperfect, she *had*, he *had*, they *had*, they *have*
passed already long before the next name appears, pluperfect
meaning the verb perfected, completed, no these persons
incomplete, they had so many years left to live, imperfect
reality, too many incomplete completed persons, etymology of
plethora says excess water in the body, no, too lurid this burial
by sea, utter the river of infinite names, end, fin, et, intended,
tender, O tend these fragile names, how sweet to see in this next
world seven-year-old _____ walking to school in Mexico City,
we dreamed of _____'s pink hair and Doc Martens boots and
her camp paintings of cats and a woman twerking, we dreamed
of _____, she had a masters degree in tourism, we dreamed
of an entire underworld district where they could finally walk
in peace, the girls and women, ni una menos, you can hear the
radio astrology of _____ wafting over infernal airwaves, no
this misguided invention, obscene to imagine that fantasy can
etch in the footage overexposed by trauma's light, no, then shall
we simply let the obituaries dictate, dox ache, dictee, dictator,
poor _____ and _____ both mayors and even young students
_____ and _____ arriving here same day alongside so many
more dispatched by Philippines police, in Brazil the polícia
followed _____ and found him as he left his church and tonight
O tonight, let us dream of Marielle Franco, who asked how
many more, I had not known you could assassinate the rainbow,

não é não, no, not, stop, halt here the travesty of poetry, the
Splenda and technicolor of lyric idealism, wrap yourself against
hurricanoes and march against the harsh tundra of reality,
shall we say that 1,600 Chinese enter the afterlife everyday
straight from work, that we saw Xu Lizhi leap out his window
and fly, levitate, levity, more morbid cuteness, when does one
stop, dozed won step, drone wind sets, Abdulrahman eating
lunch with the other boys laughing, his mop of hair, his dorky
smile, Harry Potter book in his backpack, how he came to
Hades two weeks after his father and a few years before his
sister Nawar, terribly cute, Minnie Mouse bow and tulle skirt,
a mischievous smile, No, no no no please, O please relent
the mania of mourning! We need a grief nonproliferation
treaty! _____ winner of South African suit against principal
who bullied her bathroom transphobic,,,, _____ who fought
Uganda homophobic legacy of Rule Britannia and American
evangelicals,, _____ who dreamed the qurbojoog could return,
she came alongside _____ the journalist and _____ Mogadishu
mayor, and now over the water came laughter and happy shouts,
we clapped for three weddings in Haska Meyna, Helmand, and
Wech Baghtu, no the attacks on these families were not jubilant
please stop and revoke this masque, shatter now the human
funeral and wake, wake, yes the wake, the festive crescendo of
a globe's loud grief, no, please, no, _____ the boy who swam in
Palestine, _____ who drove to his sister's wedding, no, a name
spits only paltry reduction, yes but doesn't more description
simply recite the violence once more,,, and look here comes
_____, the murdered journalist, he who stepped into the
embassy and wrote no more. .

I had waded into the Information and come back dragging a
haul of names. Still soaked, they marked a trail in the sand
behind me as I dragged them from the River. I inspected each

name and mounted them in the bezels of the text. When
I returned today, I found that almost all of the names had
vacated their positions. Their departure left only a pale shadow
on the page. Did the absence feel wet to the touch or desiccated?
I rubbed my ring finger on the white spaces and honestly could
not tell. Had the page become tainted by forgetting? Or shall we
simply say that names no longer weighed down by life quickly
evaporate.
By the Oceans of Styx, we sat,
we wept when we remembered.
We read the psalm about the rivers of Babylon,
this poem of exiles who walk
where I imagined Babel Tower splintered into rivulets
     heteroglossiac.
The poem sings that singing is impossible.
Let my tongue cling to the roof of my mouth.
Shall we halt, stop, and sigh?
Shall we stutter our melodies mute staccato?
Yes, oui, we, yes we say no more,
their souls evaporated from the page,
we say no more, they have left,
a name is no tether to kite the dead billowing
back into life. We hung our harps
upon the willows.

(We / I) invite (you / we) to the Eden of We. What is We?
We are against fungibility, tool for dolor, but for (the 99% / purse
scent / multiple personality disorder). Before the 19th century,
     those
who exhibited (multiple personality disorder / capitalism) were
thought to be possessed by a "religion of sensuous appetites."
Spiritual possession is a property relation.
We believe in ghosts, opinions we (used / use) to possess ourselves.

Possessing opinions is for posting ghosts on Twitter.
We make ghosts by (making a) killing
((via possession / via possession of (dollars / dolor))).
(Morality / Capitalism), a process poem where all nouns are
replaced by (We / money). Poetry is "economy"—artificial
   scarcity
designed to inflate meaning.
> Making we the subject of your requests effectively takes
the emphasis off you and what you get out of it.
Were the symptoms of multiple
personality disorder suggested by the questioner?
> Who asks?
Who are we when We are 70% more likely than We to find our
homes foreclosed?
We are possessed.

IV. HORIZONS

We saw a man who raised his arms in a cross.
We came closer. We greeted he whose reach marked horizon.
When he introduced himself as Delbert, he explained how
he and his comrades had cast off the planters' titles
and adopted the surname "Africa," family as capacious
as a continent. Many years ago, Delbert had stood up
from the rubble shirtless, Christ crowned with dreadlocks,
young god of the beautiful passion
whose face the helmet strikes. Yes, it was when he raised his
   arms
that they struck him, the police who'd slung siege battalions
and hosed the deluge of water cannons against
a few hippie kids, the MOVE members hated nukes
and loved animals, they'd nurtured 48 dogs
on Osage Avenue, the home at which the cops lobbed

two bombs from their chopper. When we ask him
how he came to this place, Delbert laughs.
Four decades aged in prison, he was paroled this January,
the ugly snows having soaked his young beard gray.
He lifted his arms to reprise
his famous pose, old Rasta
met by his daughter.
Only to arrive in the afterlife.
He'd survived Frank Rizzo, not cancer of prostate
and bone. But that was not the end.
He spoke of Debbie and Janine Africa
and others free and still alive and how he endured
the cruel and single cage. In solitary, Delbert had heard a tap
followed by echoes, tap against pipes,
tap tap the metal bars. Did you know you can talk
without even speaking tap tap? *Revolution being not theory
but activity.* They had taught themselves
the knock code. Knuckles too weak to batter
rude walls could still erode the loneliness.
His friends tapped
their untongued language, they asked him
riddles of Black past.
Tap, tap. What year was *Brown v. Board*?
What did John Brown do? Tap, tap.
And he heard the soft telegraph of their hands,
and he found himself
less alone. Tap, tap.
Tap.

And perhaps
we should not simply say *so many*—
maybe mourning makes more than grief—
morning that glows from dawn's fresh movements.
We have seen so many risen up,

we have seen the uprising resurrect you back
onto the soles of your feet, the cresting waves pour forth
the insurrection of we
who demand the liberation
of the air.

And that word we drape ourselves in, "we"—
does it simply name those who will one day
turn cold-bodied, we the future ghosts?
Then let me not be a ghost alone,
let us be ghosts together, old souls haunting
and coming ghosts dystopian!
Yes Beta Cáceres left
the Gualcarque river and came here, yes,
but on the same day she had welcomed a comrade
who'd come all the way from Chiapas.
"Beta Cáceres did not die, she multiplied."
Mourning like *we*
is a style of love.
We dream of people.
The *we* we lost,
remember the horror yes the iniquity,
and remember too the *we*
we wish to be.
We who dreamed that Sarah Hegazy forgave the world.
So let us whisper one last wish "against the great defeat
of the world," let our song send one last huff
funneling into soggy lungs struggling
to resuscitate.

Intimate democracy is seeing the back of your head!
We march!
March the month the lockdown started!

March the singing step of cement and no transcendence!
March the exodus opposite of occupation!
Occupation, what so many no longer possess.
Vocation, vocare, a calling, to call awake that mythical beast, the
    people rousing.
Sing the yawn and steam of your mouths sweet!
We is where seduction is irrelevant—would I whisper sweet
    nothings to your back?
O intimate democracy, I know you as well as the back of your
    head.

....

.. ..

... ...

.. ..

V. CYNICAL GEOGRAPHIES

Dawn tumbling, a new day's light refracting prismatic
through wet mourning. Already almost waking, we walk through
fields of black tires burning, plains where they flame metal.
The men sprint their four-tired wheelbarrows, they farm the
    bounty
of Agbogbloshie's dead machines. We see them
draw cursive fire from the loops of copper wire
and the yarn of USB. We see the television sets
already snuffed, fumigated of its luminous ghosts.
We see the cairns stacked from calculator, Palm Pilot, pager,
Betamax, antique future bric-a-brac.
Global dump outside Accra
where they bannered the black star first.
Here is where we wake up,

the men say nothing and stoke the bonfires.
We wake smelling the thick soot, modernity's ashes:
more turf
from these metal smoldering fields.

Half dreaming where the Hades terroir
slopes into our human geographies, we stepped
into the mosque they built in Babur's reign,
early modern helipad for alighting angels.
They say you could hear a single whisper under its
three majestic domes, but who can hear anything over
the shouting, the chanting, the hammering,
now that the unruly kar sevaks have scaled the mosque
and stand upon it, a hateful crew manning
the deck of some terrible ship, dark vessel cleaving
forth the waters towards a dead future.
Modernity's just a rumor for mobs, tumor
of supremacists, whose demolition has transposed
the Ayodhya temple to this universal necropolis.
Here it still exists, an unruin,
uncontested by the saffron flags
the fascists left, no longer infested
by howling monkeys.
Freedom means being squatters
on seemingly impossible lands: Kashmir Azadi!
Almost 300 mosques and shrines killed in Gujarat alone,
like the tomb of this poet, who vandals buried
a second time beneath tar.
Poor Wali Gujarati, old Sufi romantic bulldozed
long after passing. We dreamed his shrine pierced
the shabby asphalt road, we saw it shoot up
like a rocket while we recited
his words, *O how our love*
has melted the despots!

VI. LINE OF REFLECTION

Whittle ourselves a moment into more intimate we.
We had been sunbathing when my wife's father
recited a poem by Paul Valery.
What did it mean?
Who knows? I don't speak French!
My wife's mother supplied the title, "The Symmetry of the Sea."
Was the poet talking about the fertility of still water,
whose mere skin can reproduce the world?
Today, the cresting and lick of la mer crumble away
all mirrors. I could not reflect.
I gazed sunburnt toward less perfect duplications.
1) The blue swath painted by the ocean's stroke.
2) The pale lunar plain, bathers whose drowsy bareness
illuminated the sand.
Two horizons! Did you know that the flounder's eye
migrates from one side of its head
to the other? This flatfish that Levi-Strauss called
the beast of binary thinking.
Water and also land.
Those who live, those who have passed.
We ate sliced pink peaches, purple grapes,
and watermelon balls. My mother-in-law repeated herself
and I heard what I had refused to hear:
"The Cemetery by the Sea."
We had buried my father in a cemetery
that calls itself a "memorial park."
The phrase suggests strange recreations.
Wait, maybe I'm mishearing again,
how is it possible
to possess symmetry with the dead?
Yes, memory is reflection.
What we remember

replaces what remains.
Cemetery (sic) suggests that a figure remains
even after each rotation. Where am I?
Where are we? It can be hard to say
when the surf retracts the planet
from your feet. The waves return.
The waves do not cleanse the world,
they strip meat from the beached whale
heaving to breathe. We hold our hands, we run,
we leap into the waters.

Isola

J. MAE BARIZO

J. MAE BARIZO

Born in Toronto to Filipino immigrants, **J. MAE BARIZO** is the author of *The Cumulus Effect* (Four Way Books). A poet, essayist, and performer, recent work appears or is forthcoming in *Poetry, Ploughshares, Boston Review, Esquire,* and *Los Angeles Review of Books*. She is the recipient of fellowships and awards from Bennington College, the New School, Jerome Foundation, and Poets House. An advocate of cross-genre collaboration, her song cycles "Chroma" and "Isola" will be premiered at Princeton University in Fall 2020. She teaches at the New School and Pratt Institute and lives in New York City.

Lux Aeterna

That morning again you hauled my arm to the window
and put a new dress on it. Let me, you said.
The street machines were singing and how young
we were and always eating. Buying food
at the bodegas, fleshy Jewish rolls, nectarines, skin-tight
plums. The way that day you held the phone
like a baby but it wouldn't stay still. Because the sky
was white, the streets were white and your hands
had me all over them. Because the light was blonde
the way we liked the boys then. Before
the curfews, before the sheltered dark. Tell me
that I remember it correctly, that the light
will lick and lick the damage clean. That it is not
ruin already. Tell me.

Sunday Women on Malcolm X Boulevard

My lungs grow black lilies
while I play Bach's *Ich ruf zu dir*

on the spinet in the Harlem room.
The light is getting longer

and the one love I keep hoarding
is still asleep while wildfires

bloom a few miles away. He too
must be locked in a room full

of music, waking slow. From
my window I can see inside

other chambers where my sisters
read the news of melting ice-caps

and the virus named after a crown;
other mothers and daughters tending

their small plunders. They wonder
how long to hold onto husbands, how

to skin a chicken, how to tend a fire
that burns thousands of miles away.

I breathe, alveoli burning, many-petaled
in the dark. As a child I used to stick

my finger into the flower's stamen
and lick, orange powder searing

my lips. See how my desire thrives?
Feeding on every living thing.

The Mothers

We must be
the inviolate
petals, always
queering to-
wards the sun,
must be water
on the lips of
flaming cities,
quenching
the husbands,
insatiable. These
days the abdomen
blossoms, but
we must be
boneless, edible
fish. We must
beg for bouquets
for absent sons.
This is how we
know devotion:
listening to lovers
sleep, breathing
like monster trucks,
wanting to soothe
them when the dream
is done. We march
the sinking avenues,
finger the curls
at the baby's neck,
hanging from
the brink at

office hour,
gulping Xanax
in their white
oblong shells.
Clouds can sleep
but we can never.
Vigilant animals
on our hands and
knees, asking for
it again and again.

Survival Skills (Small Essay on Extinction)

Being able to dodge
a bullet, eat kale

with gusto, avoid
gluten altogether.

I couldn't decide
whether I should

stay or run faster—
how to be faithful?

Do genes play
a factor? Were

my ancestors
concubines or slaves?

The longer desire
takes to find an outlet

the less it can be contained.
Consider the fermata

in a sonata, practicing
always for disappearance

New York, November

Today, my restless, yellow leaves are thrashing
through the wind. The air in this city is thick
with fear and want and every day the men and
women start to build again. Our lives, as we keep
track of them, are acted out in simple gestures: hand
to mouth, a gasp, a clear-cut kiss, or not. Nothing
harmful, nothing said. The things we never speak of
are like the lost debris, or yellow leaves in any city,
any fall. But something tells us this is different. Maybe
it's that sad, burnt scent without a name. Perhaps
it's just New York, miles from where you are. All
I can really be sure of these days are the words
I write you from my crowded heart, and the yellow
leaves, and the way one season meets the next, violently.

At the Whitney, Thinking About the Trees

Impossible to ignore, the trees. You were alone
in a hospital bed, probably in an immodest gown.
Siri said—*distance is a vector quantity; distance is a primal
fact*—I was so afraid then of death that I kept silent,
eating continuously. At the museum there were no
names on the artwork; I kept taking pictures of clouds.
Would I love you more if you died? I wanted the future
to be uncertain because I was tired of being unsurprised.
Did you save the gif of me falling into the lake? You
were silent on social media. I googled "I'm so mysterious
I can't even understand myself." *Distance is displacement
distance is measured in* ... In the museum, I wanted
to touch everything on the walls. Look, a bleeding
cloud. A stranger was sewing up your incision. On
the screen the trees and their thousand petal tongues.

View from an Apartment

Scissored clouds with light snaking
through. Masks and jumpers, footsteps
like ants in a flurry. She craved bodegas
and foreign films. To walk out of a building
and squint, surprised by so many words.
There was wind outside, trees swaying
like uncertain eyelids. Sidewalks
and sun as it struck them. She knew
that what was written was meant
to be forgotten. *Sometimes I sing so pretty
it breaks my own heart.* She was humming
into the hemisphere but no one
could hear it. Outside the pedestrians
gleamed like pinpricks. Someone
somewhere was walking away.

Isola

one sense of sleep
is the disappearance
of the eyes

perceiving in afternoon
a slit in the texture

one day maybe
not soon i'll be able
to take trains

*

today i will put the blanket
out again

even with the coffee spill
the sunlight tenders

my skin

*

i dream of taxi cabs

isolation comes from the word "isola"

venus retrogrades
and all the not-yet-lovers
come slithering back

*

i wonder where the light went

the orange light

"it's more bearable to think of death than of love"

lying on the grass
with a milk coffee
thinking about my mother

her malignant nerve

*

(in my dreams
i am sent back
to the trenches

cold trucks
on the avenue

marking borders)

*

i lay the blanket
on the grass
but it is wet still

did i leave the books
out too long

to sanitize?

i was supposed
to be writing
about time

(lungs
in tiny cabinets)

remembering
how someone
looked at you

will there
be islands?

noise
at the center?

the now of remembering

of the future memory
of the future passed

Time Trying

DORA MALECH

DORA MALECH is the author of four books of poems, most recently *Flourish* (Carnegie Mellon University Press, 2020) and *Stet* (Princeton University Press, 2018). In 2019, Eris Press published *Soundings*, a UK Selected of Malech's poems and drawings. Her poems have appeared in the *New Yorker*, *Poetry*, *The Best American Poetry*, and numerous other publications. She is the recipient of awards that include an Amy Clampitt Residency Award, a Ruth Lilly Poetry Fellowship, a Mary Sawyers Baker Prize, and a Writer's Fellowship from the Civitella Ranieri Foundation. She has been a Visiting Artist at the American Academy in Rome and a Distinguished Writer-in-Residence at Saint Mary's College of California. She lives in Baltimore, where she is an assistant professor in The Writing Seminars at Johns Hopkins University.

Dream Recurring

All eyes turn doorward
toward me.
                    This is History.
        Where are you supposed to be?

Torah Study

At more than one synagogue, congregants received an email this week
asking them to no longer kiss the Torah scroll in reverence.
—Sarah Maslin Nir, the *New York Times*, March 9, 2020

Sweet skeptic, nonbeliever
for whom I never

wrote a vow, not wanting
to fuss and press at the us of us,

not wanting to conscript and constrict
into some narrow stripe of service,

years into this, I've found
the words and want

to recommit as such. I don't believe
that it's too much to ask. Here goes.

My atheist, may I die,
some distant day, your holy

book, your sacred text: ancient,
full of poetry, and often kissed.

Tried

on the floor before
a party at which
no one thought

much about shared air
the virus still elsewhere
or we thought the virus

still a far fear
and my body
telling me it

was time to try
I won't go into
detail a certain

detail was my body
telling me to try and
the calendar agreed

we call it a window
let's try in the window
as if it's public work

spectacle like we have
a show to show for our
effort or wares to display

funny to think of February's
as the year's last parties
leap we say as if we're

trying to urge it all over all
evening I drank fizzy water
and tried to believe in cells

like those bubbles
something going
are you trying are

you trying are you
trying bright inside
of me and beyond

lay the lie lodged deep
in believe and the sting
of a thing that could be

History

I felt I carried something in me
and cared for it accordingly

with vitamins and pride. I won't
say what I named it, but I named it

out loud. Then, no heartbeat.
Whatever it was wasn't and never

was. Don't look at me with pity.
You know you've known

its name and how it feels to hold
inside you and believe it to be

good, and growing, only to learn
that it was nothing all along.

Nothing, but much bloodier.

Iris Park

How many times have I typed
"dead" for "dear" this spring?
Enough. My loss, less art than
craft this spring, a name spelled

out in uncooked noodles and glue
pitched in the kitchen trash,
construction paper steeped in dregs,
bent corner dabbing at potatoes' eyes,

ripped edge wicking the last juice
from a brown core. Outside,
rain is pestering the little
leaves again and flooding

the road my mind drives back
north to the hospital, where each
precast concrete parking structure
is named after a flower.

After "After Us"

Others' pity will set out after us
like the moon after some wandering child.
—Nikola Madzirov

Nikola, I owe you a note. So many *one day*s in a row
for so many. To answer, finally, I am as fine as anyone
could hope to be within a system's spinning.
I spent a season and another and another watching:
    the neighbor's shows through her window,
    the cases climbing—red bolts of data
        and the rumble that follows,
        dissonant chord of lies and prayers,
    my mouth.
Held tongue chafes, no balm but these same seasons,
embraceless despite the over-armed police.
You begin to end in a last kind wish for me and mine:
   I do hope—
and from afar I borrow a bit of what I need
as any neighbor might, with thanks—

Dear Nikola,
    I do hope too.

After "The Day After My Father's Death"

to keep the other children safe
from my infectious grief
they left me in lockdown
—Bill Knott

Explain quarantine to children,
says the headline. If they could
read, we could leave the truth
lying around for them to trip
over, but these little ones are
still blank and shiny as their own
wet thumbs, so we say
this is a one-time thing.
We're near the end.
We can see them again soon,
meaning each missed
someone. Soon, near, one,
can, we say. Those were the
generic words the mini-mart
had, so we stocked up quick,
watched rain drip off the roof.

How to Make It

All my friends are now at a distance,
overwhelmed with work and world and care,

injustice, filled with fear of bills and illness,
running scared though going nowhere and so,

of course, taking on more chores by other
names: some contorting toward the E chord on

their new mail-order ukulele fretboards,
others wielding hooks and needles to pull

hats and scarves from skeins of yarn through spring
and into summer, or coddling green fleets

of cotyledons to life in hope of herbs
and flowers, yes, but also just to tend

some simpler lives writ bright in potting soil,
and one with palms planted easing her knees

up her shaking arm toward side crow pose,
another shaking shots and ice and adding

-tini or -rita to each concoction's end,
and another beating cream of tartar

into egg whites aspiring to alpine
range as part one of step two of nine

in a thirteen-ingredient recipe
to bake the perfect homemade yodel cake, while

elsewhere behind my own closed door I restart
the video of Yodel 101

with yodeler Wylie Gustafson who makes
a song out of the place we break over and

over again. What luck each time he asks
me *to warm up with a dejected sigh.*

Missed Miscarriage

Term of crumpled paper scrawled with false
starts in this essay we will in this essay

we will this term to mean more than the sum
of its partitions no say ramifications

for its roots in branches as in plant
a flag and sow the soil ours poll pole

as no fixed point to guide us but a trunk
running rings or stuffed with plunder plant

a flag and it grows each limb as consequence
to ramify again one letter's foothills

swapped at birth for a cross and tendered to
the touch to ratify a term that never

looked inside to see that it was made
of its own ending now how can we claim

we didn't feel its onus in us this
missed miscarriage of that which we willed our

ears to mishear *just is* swore our oath on
a book of holes wore that tight dress we claimed

in white and gold when all along the truth
was black and blue as any other region

of injury just a striped piece of cloth
aloft but enough to show our shape proudly

hate to make this figure belong to a body
but it's what's still on hand and what we have

our hands on still inside us justice stilled
inside us missed miscarriage of now and

how can we say that this was never ours
or anything that we once wanted when

we have carried it in us for so long

Animal Crossing

I.

> In my dreams
> the snouts drool on the marble,
> suffering children, suffering flies,
> suffering the consumers
> who won't meet their steady eyes
> for fear they could see.
> —Philip Levine, "Animals Are Passing from Our Lives"

I've never played it, but I've seen
the game's name everywhere this spring,
though by everywhere I really
mean the screens where I sought solace
when the pandemic pushed us all
inside. The name repeats inside
my brain, rifling through for loose
referents, fair game, and finds

Midwestern penguins wandering
not free but freer through the empty
halls of closed aquariums
and museum galleries, taking
in the glint off schools of fish
and Venetian altarpieces,

the hopeful hoax dolphins supposedly
swimming the canals of Venice,
or rather, the real dolphins
filmed in the Mediterranean
hundreds of miles from the bronze lion

spreading his centuries-old wings
over Piazza San Marco,

the Bronx Zoo's flesh-and-blood lions
and tigers symptomatic, coughing
dry coughs, refusing to eat, testing
positive for the not-animal
of the virus replicating
its seemingly insatiable
not-appetite to not-live on,

the red knot sandpipers headed
toward the Arctic hungry this May,
their usual horseshoe crab egg feast
on the shores of the Delaware Bay
foiled by this year's colder water
and storm-slowed spawning,

and the rows of horseshoe crabs
just inland inside the Lonza biotech
facility, steel needles draining
bottles of their milky blue blood
for its primeval sensitivities,
as any vaccine made for us will
need to pass their ancient assay first.

II.

    A gray light coming on at dawn,
    No fresh start and no bird song
    And no sea and no shore
    That someone hasn't seen before.
    —Philip Levine, "A New Day"

Finally venturing out again in June,
I sing my way across the Bay Bridge,

radio up and windows down.
I get some distance, keep my distance.
Shells and telsons litter the littoral
zone, a little literal litter
too, a plastic bag that echoes
THANK YOU, which I pincer
gingerly between my thumb
and forefinger to trek back up
across the hot sand and toss
in the bins by the dunes. The rest
I see, I leave. I'm sweaty from
my one good deed. Pelicans skim
in formation. One tern returns another's
reprimand. Later I hang my
clothes on the line, but nothing dries
completely this close to the sea.

III.

> Somewhere beyond the Flood
> We wandered hand in hand
> In a country we remember
> Somewhere in our blood . . .
> —Philip Levine, "Who Are You?"

I confess that this is not a game
and should be over, but I don't
know how long it takes to play
what's not a game. I admit I asked
the neighbor's clumsy cat if any
body can live on feathers alone
as she crouched against
my steps again below the
round mouths of the perfect
holes the carpenter bees keep

boring because even my wooden
railing remains unfinished.

The Kaddish never mentions death,
but we know when we need to say it,
the Viddui too, confession,
though there's no confession in
the Hebrew Bible as a noun,
not something but something to do,
for example, to lay hands
upon the head of a living goat
and confess a nation's sins upon it.

The copyrighted syllables
run on, chyronic elegy
on the head-in-handheld
disconsolate console of my mind,
shibboleth-for-one each time
that rhythm is or isn't in
my sights, its stresses landing heavy
on its "a" and "cross" with the rest
of each word padding obediently
behind. The belts and hooks begin
again to bear the bodies and
the parts of bodies past the workers
standing shoulder to shoulder for
our appetites, the virus lingering
in the frigid indoor air,
the virus hitching a ride home
on company buses, belying the execs'
beliefs in their versions of processing
and of power, in plastic and in palatable
names—those first tests on animals

performed in Eden's biotech facility—
those sounds we made with our own
mouths to put things in their place,
those mouths of ours that now—still
now—are even deadly when we sing.

photographs from

The Infinite Present

B. A. VAN SISE

LACEY TREADWAY

B. A. VAN SISE is an internationally known photographer and the author of the award-winning visual poetry anthology, *Children of Grass*. His visual work has previously appeared in the *New York Times*, *Village Voice*, *Washington Post* and *BuzzFeed News*, as well as in major museum exhibitions throughout the United States, including Ansel Adams' Center for Creative Photography, the Peabody Essex Museum, the Museum of Jewish Heritage, and the Smithsonian's National Portrait Gallery. His written work has appeared in 2020 in *Poets & Writers*, the *Southampton Review*, *Eclectica*, and the *North American Review*.

Photographs, like poems, require presence—both in our own lives and our own surroundings.

The Japanese have a term, *mono no aware* (物の哀れ), literally the *pathos of things*: We must understand that nothing, not one thing in the dazzling circus of our time here, is permanent. Not a pandemic, not a civil war, not a love, not a life. All of our moments are present ones.

A photograph, a poem, a memory, these are thieves of time: the taking of a temporary instant to turn it into permanent ephemera. In this year of trials, perhaps, the memory of the exhausting world is not what anyone wants, but might be what so many need: to be forced, yearning in isolation, our hands and mouths and lips and hearts six feet apart, to find the poetry in the pain, and carry it on with us.

For the last three years, I have defined my pathos of things by making one and only one film photograph, every day, with no do-overs and no second chances; through much of the early stages of the pandemic, I abandoned my flailing, native New York for the American South and Southwest, spending three months on the road, making one photograph daily, slewing around the continent watching a well-warned but unsuspecting South as it stepped hesitantly into presence in the national nightmare.

Film photographs are indelible; making one photograph daily, one does not see the results for months at a time. Few of these images are the ones I expected to see—but in reality history, like poetry, never seems to turn out the way it's planned: Truth is rarely the same as memory.

These are some of this year's photographs, from our increasingly infinite present.

Pandemia

JON DAVIS

JON DAVIS is the author of five chapbooks and six full-length poetry collections, most recently *An Amiable Reception for the Acrobat* (Grid Books, 2019). His seventh collection, *Above the Bejeweled City*, is forthcoming from Grid Books in 2021. Davis also co-translated Iraqi poet Naseer Hassan's *Dayplaces* (Tebot Bach, 2017). He has received a Lannan Literary Award, the Lavan Prize from the Academy of American Poets, the Off the Grid Poetry Prize, and two National Endowment for the Arts Fellowships. He taught for 23 years at the Institute of American Indian Arts before founding, in 2013, the IAIA low-residency MFA in Creative Writing, which he directed until his retirement in 2018. From 2013 to 2015, he served as the City of Santa Fe's fourth Poet Laureate.

Ode to the Coronavirus

Teach me how to love the cough, the test,
the social distance, canceled prom, empty gym,

the steady slide into impoverishment.
My ears, at this late age, make of silence

a steady hiss, so I'm never alone, except
with my failures. Failure to forget myself

completely for just a moment. Even as
my granddaughter swings her tiny foot—*golpe,*

golpe, golpe—I'm thinking *my* granddaughter, as if
the reckless joy she brings to the dance

is part mine. But nothing is mine. And that's
the lesson you came to teach. Everything

crumbling. Everything suspended a moment
like pollen on the water at the top of a waterfall.

Or like a stray dog in traffic, lunging & turning.
Or a bat in the bedroom flapping raggedly

toward one wall & the next. If just for one
moment I could still the hiss in my ears,

the shuddering in my chest, or call it
something else—a *shimmering*—then would I be

like the humming stones at the waterfall's foot
that welcome the weight of water & pollen:

golpe fuerte, golpe de suerte, golpe mortal.

Choose Your Own America

for Dean Rader

You can choose the forefathered one,
all beard and stovepipe, folderol
and feather, all foppish at the brothel.
Or that earlier one, all lunge and gallop,
musket and scatter, belfry and blunderbuss.
Or the gangrenous and stooped one, caterwauling
on the White House lawn. You can choose
the haunted one, nightshakes, the guilt-worn
and riddled, still moaning in the willows.
Or the exuberant one, the one that prances—
gray squirrel on an electrical wire,
all pomp and reflex, tail toss and brass.
Then there's the worried one, furtive
in the hovel, the duckers and shamblers,
scriveners of the mud's cursive. Or the America
of duplicates and editions, of ranch houses
and khakis, quick pledge and the concrete walkway.
You can choose the America of granite,
of cobblestone, of quick strike and vanish.
Or the America of *gracias* in the market,
miigwech on the subway, never mind
the sleek traders on the balcony, the champagne
they drizzle on the occupying hordes below.

State of the Union

Meanwhile, the endless marketing of insinuations:
The headphoned man, the Fox News crawl,
the economy in its blue suit, each slaughter
a selling point, each tongue slip unleashing
a delirium of pundits, a gloating, a tweetstorm,
a chance to vanquish.
                    The choices were cabernet
or chardonnay. The charcuterie was shuttered.
The engine sounded most confident—full-throated
and steady—to the passengers over the wing.
Elsewhere, a thin humming, a mosquito
in a sleeper's ear. Elsewhere, the undisciplined roar.
Elsewhere, the shifts and vicissitudes. The man
and woman on the tiny screen, rebuilt
in their own image, would live forever now,
limned and animated, death bringers
in the uncanny valley. We slid over the land
as if on a thin layer of grief. The celebration
was nested inside the fatalities, the cordoned
holocaust.
            This was the American Way,
the music seeping into the lobby like radiation.
One word for it might be *obsequious*. Another,
vainglorious. As in that caravanned orchestra
mounted on white horses that serenaded
Custer's 25th Cavalry, until arduousness
trumped ardor and they turned back.
In the soundtrack of our days, history manifests
as fatuous strings, the fortissimo of empire
swelling, filling the silence until even the victims
are humming along.

                    Until one black man kneels,
another begins clapping. Until a single black woman
leans back, her eyes squeezed shut
against the moment's misery, and lets loose
something between sob and howl.
                                        We live
now in that arc between signal and noise,
that sparkleap, that wail beseeching justice,
that craw-engendered cry shaped by lungs and tongue,
lips and teeth, such keening set loose in the murderous world.

Brief

You arrived eager, full of expectation,
But I was a dull host, neither ripe flesh
Nor fodder, and you drifted and probed,
Divining a vacant chemistry. Absent
Of your absinthe, I was poor meat.

What you'd wanted was something else.
What you got was too much human.
Your path, a meandering red line.
Aimless, aware your time was brief, you
Swerved in the russet of your conundrum.

Did I entice, encourage? Very well,
I enticed. You, who would have—
Had I been elsewise—set spur to flesh
And got purchase on a future. I regret
The role I played in that deception.

Like a cat, I leaned in the sunny tropics,
And you mistook me and launched
Your sally. I was wrong for you;
You, wrong for me. But there was
No escape. I stopped you then—

Your misery which seemed the brink
Of pleasure—and felt your fluttering,
Lurching trip to nowhere cease. Old
Companion, I miss you, though even now
Cannot parse symptom from disease.

Western Civ

—pre-dawn, St. Pierre des Champs

Whatever owls and storks inhabit this town are still. No
nightingales warble and trill. I cross the meadow and the Orbieu
River and climb toward the stone and shuttered town. My own
sharp footsteps. A few thin lights. No traffic. No one but me out
walking. It occurs to me that I don't know the dangers here.
But they've had centuries to clear the landscape of poisons,
shoot the dangerous animals and display them in the town
square. And by now the race of evil men John Locke wanted to
protect us from has surely been reduced to a reclusive, shamed
population on an island somewhere. The night is mostly a dark
vagueness. The night is mostly imagined, a thin cobblestone
street curving between stone buildings. Buildings built and
rebuilt and added to. The layers of history. The shop now a
bed & breakfast, the pasture, a campground. Mostly, though, a
settled beauty: narrow streets, houses, an occasional lit window,
lace curtains, nobody awake reading Proust on the divan or
slicing truffles and parmesan in the kitchen. Where the road
edges the river, an engine idles, three men smoke and talk
softly, in utter darkness.

The Eros That Camps on the Edge of the Valley of Death Is the Only Eros

Eros of wars and gods and the hardscrabble millions. Of
pustules pox and the fire-blind saints. Of stalkers clandestine
and their backlit prey. Of monuments of wet falling snow. Of car
crash tire spin the calligraphy of blood.

Of darkness of the shadows inside darkness. Of napes and ears
of tongues and lips. Of hair brushing warm across the back of a
hand. Of teeth and nails and the hard grip. Of wrist-back knee-
back depths of the eyes.

Of leaf-tremble elk-bugle the bittern's deep bellows. Of
floodwaters plane crash high mountain stream. Of whiteout
blizzard of snowblind and lost. Of firelight smoke-spire eyes
deep in shadow. Of now now now. Of always. Of never. Of long
darkness and the one bright flash.

In the Tumultuous Dawn

In the tumultuous dawn—
    Turk's cap lilies,
        chatter of finches,
            sun-glint off the silver roof.

Unhomed by theory,
    alienated from this plenty,
        you prop the wooden palette
           against the cardboard

that holds the tarp
    so the accumulated rain
        pours off the downslope side.

Somebody's cheap boombox
    squeals and rumbles "in
        the government yard
          in Frenchtown"
            then fades.

Soon, you will storm the palace.
    Soon the tear gas.
        The LRAD.
          The water cannons.

Even this is an industry.
    Even this feeds capital.
        Even your resistance is monetized.

Only the warbler flickering
   in the greenery is of no consequence—
    feathery nihilist in the nada
     of palmetto and plume.

The Body is the Site of Discipline

"No moment is innocent."
—Carolyn Huber

We are formed by trauma and torment,
a system of punishments and rewards
(which are also punishments).

Pleasure is a kind of discipline.

Absent discipline, we languish in freedom.

Freedom is the longed-for punishment.

Nothing, the song says,
left to lose.

Ardent among box elders.
Squeamish in the barrow-pit.
Sodden among sods.

We are hogs snorting through leaf-mold,
sniffing out pleasure then
justice then pleasure again.

When we are giving pleasure,
we are half-dervish, half-devil.

To give pleasure is to tame,
to make-oneself-indispensable.

The gaze is everywhere.

In the sun room alone, among the houseplants:
the sun's gaze, the begonia's gaze,
the ticking of a clock.

Everything conspires.

Soundings

In the instructions, we are warned to decide how energetic we
    want our chorus to be—
Happening is not what we thought it was: *occurrence* vets even
    the ridgetop plume—
Empaneled now, we can see the threat clearly—
Frogs lounging, floating, stretched just under the water's
    surface, sunlight orbing the eyes, turning yellow-green all the
    edges of evolution's endangered child—
The nerves carouse even in sleep, even in the stillness before
    dawn—
Randomness is purposeful—
He wakes in pain, his neck barely able to hold up his
    beleaguered head—
Best to avoid the tonic entirely in the verse and let the tension
    build—
The dream arose in response to the day's events, but the talking
    deer in his open palm was unexpected—
The whimsical arrives as an apparent counter to death, but
    death is in everything like a secret ingredient—
Seen dispassionately, the centipede was briefly beautiful: tawny,
    mechanical, precise—
A poem's articulations, its ligatures: evolved form and
    stentorian depths—
The engine of activism is often the overbearing father, the bed
    pitched and slung, the breathing—
The three-legged tomcat returned from a night hunt to lay a
    three-legged weasel on the back step—
We attempt to distinguish between the miraculous and the
    coincidental, not realizing that the miraculous and the
    coincidental are indistinguishable—
They mined everything for meaning, as if meaning were a
    nutrient—

If all the memories return, she said, will I be the person I was
     before the accident and how will I know—
The star-nosed mole, fur slick and sheened, popped out of the
     leaf-pile and was briefly gunmetal-gray and beautiful and
     ill-made for travel over grass—
Your lyrics in the bridge should resolve whatever issues the
     verse and chorus raised—
About is always an illusion, a mask: so much energy given
     over, given up, given, as in this gift of quiet: the wren
     pausing, tilting its head, the cat a mirrored silence in the
     bunchgrass—

Vintage

for Maxine

The singer sang a cappella for 30 seconds and then the beat
    dropped.
Now where were we? We kept talking about that cute thing
our granddaughter did. The kids wanted to talk about the failure
of cryptocurrency to capture the public's imagination.
Then we remembered the "kids" were thirty-something. The actual
kids were speaking a language we didn't recognize at all. We were
binge-watching our days and they were terrifying—pandemics,
deaths by cancer, inexplicable deaths, deaths of birds trembling
beside the plate glass. We kept voting for the least-offensive
    politician.
But we were governed by a shrill posse from up near the treeline.
It was spring, and the finches were copulating in the peach tree
but it didn't cheer us. The skunks ambled through the arugula
like mental patients. We couldn't remember the name
of that disease that kept you from remembering. We couldn't
remember the name of the person we could call who would know.
We were googling it, typing into our phones with a single
shaking finger. Looking over then through our glasses.
All the knowledge we had acquired no longer applied—
the past tense of *lie*, where the semicolon went, the past tense
of *lead*, how to calculate fractions, the capital of Idaho.
How had we been so wrong about the future? No jet packs
but all these algorithms. Everything extruded. Everything we
    loved
now *vintage*. Yet still, in isolated pockets, people were making
    music
on actual instruments. Still, in isolated pockets, actual food
    from gardens.
In the swamps, actual frogs, harrumphing in the cattails,

redwings trilling and spreading their wings, a lone heron
drifting ghostly above its ghostlier reflection, and somebody's
granddaughter hunkered in the mud, saying "wait," saying "frogs,"
just crouched and still, just listening to our vintage world.

Above the Bejeweled City

I was a guest in their house. A house
set at the lit edge of a great city. Below us
a virus was floating like dust motes
through the streets. Their daughter
had raised a jarful of butterflies—
not a jar exactly, more like a vase.
I was having drinks with them in violation
of the latest edicts from the premier.
When they weren't speaking to me
they spoke a bright guttural language
like the one you might imagine
river rocks would speak
at the bottom of a mountain stream.
At one point in the evening,
the daughter rose politely from her chair
and performed a kind of flamenco,
snaking her hands into the air as if
pulling herself through dense undergrowth.
How can I explain? The world was ending.
In the city below people were collapsing,
struggling to breathe. I didn't know why
there were fires or why smoke
marbled the sky above the buildings.
I tried to imagine individual deaths,
eyes looking out from behind glass visors,
hands reaching up to be held.
It seemed the least I could do.
We moved onto the balcony
that overlooked the city.
We brought the vase of butterflies.
Flashing red lights jeweled the streets below us.

Sirens flared and stopped and flared again.
We stood quietly in the darkness.
As I understood it, my host was
a professor of some rarely spoken language.
His wife sang cabaret songs in a local bistro.
We removed the cover of the vase
and released the butterflies.
Would you believe me if I told you
that they sprang from the jar as though
forced upward by a burst of air, and
that they did not flutter away into the night
but one by one landed on that girl
until she was covered with wings,
all gently pulsing? Oh, readers,
it was lovely there on that balcony
above the dying world. And for a moment,
I thought she might step away
and leave the butterflies hanging there
in the shape of a girl.
After a while she pointed to herself.
What's happening? she whispered.
Her parents said something
in their underwater language
that caused her to begin slowly turning,
and the butterflies began to loosen their grip
and flutter into the night,
catching the light a moment
before they were lost in the general darkness.
*That is how it has always been done
in our country*, my host told me.
With one such as her.
And I believed them, dear reader.
Wouldn't you have? On such a night,
in such a world—

Roommate, Woman

LEE YOUNG-JU, TRANSLATED BY JAE KIM

LEE YOUNG-JU is the author of the poetry collections *You Arrived in the Season of Perennial Summer* (2020), *Keep No Record of Love* (2019), *Cold Candies* (2014), *Sister* (2010), and *The Hundred-and-Eighth Man* (2005). She lives in Seoul, South Korea.

JAE KIM is a writer and a translator of Korean poetry. His work has recently appeared in *Conjunctions*, *Guernica*, *NOON*, *Poem-a-Day*, *Words Without Borders*, *Poetry Review*, and Action Books' Poetry in Action series. His translation of a collection of Lee Young-ju's poems is forthcoming from Black Ocean in 2021. He lives in St. Louis, Missouri.

Sister

On a winternight, I want to go from the outside to the inside.
Outside to inside, since no one's inside. Trying to go inside, I
take the handle that's cold as a knife and tear it off the door. If I
have a door handle, I'll be able to turn it, press the belly button,
or change my point of view geometrically. The damp smells
Mother has spread on the floor. There had been mushrooms I
wanted to call *Sister*, but when I woke from my sleep, Mother
was snipping, with a fruit knife, snipping their heads off.
Where should the handle go? You're down below. This strange
reaction I have of weeping whenever the inside of my body
turns dark. I want to call this damp, decaying inside *Sister*. You
put the door handle on the round mound of your mushroom
heart and have a look inside. It's the mushrooms, awake from
their slumber, snipping, snipping Mother's head off. When
you mean to go from outside to inside, when you can't find the
handle you've left outside in the dark, when the inside, where
there's no one, turns inside-out in a mushroom shape, you be-
gin to call the frosted window of Apt. 202 *Sister*.

Roommate, Woman

On waking, I see my body has been rearranged. I'm reminded of the tongue you, having cried so much, dropped under the cypress tree. From then on, you began to speak with your left hand. One of my eyes, stuck to my thigh, closed and opened toward the obsolete picture. When your ovary, full of blood, keeps moving down, you open the window. A whistle sounds. The police touches the face of the rat the cat never finished. There behind your back is my pain, isolated from my knees. You knew the house would be rearranged when we woke up—I hold your hand. While we watch the pale clouds, sitting on leaking fuel tanks, our joined hands slip out the door. You pick up one of my eyes worming under your foot. It may snow. Snow (not an eye) like the bandage around my hand, smeared in crimson light.

Mama's Marmalade

Though I leave the door open, you just don't know to come out.
Like a stone that has kneaded the sweet fruit, kneaded until
the tender, sweet-smelling flesh was completely gone. I stirred
for a long time with a long chopstick. Shall we leave? Floating
this half-question by you. Everything here will drip into your
mouth. Not rotting, but as-is. You're kneading, kneading your
own hands and feet inside the jar. I want to make you, layer by
layer, into a person who doesn't rot. Even in a moment of crying,
I pray the sweet tears may drip into the jar, so you can lick it,
and even after death, may the flesh harden when cold water
is poured, and the stone pressing upon the heart ... I could
leave the lid off, and you still won't be able to get out. Let's get
out together, I blew wind into the jar. Such a beautiful stench.
I thought it might be coming from the wind in the jar. You're
using, in place of your hands and feet, your stump of body to
suck on the fruit-flesh. What's this breeze that has leaked out of
my soul? At once, everything began to rot. Like a sitting sitter,
you just don't know to stand. The dizzying wind began here. The
room I lived in when I was twenty. Every jar on the floor was
rotting.

Guest

Foreigners are sitting. Even though it's my house, only the use of
a foreign language is allowed. A person who's lost her language,
I circle the living room. A bright steam rises from the kettle and
dissipates. A soft pitch. Languages are afloat, like feathers. Soft
wings. I stretch my hand out to catch a scurrying sound. If I lose
my meaning, can I slowly rise? Like this? What use to us are
those meanings that don't reach each other? White snow falls,
falls outside my window. I hear words I don't understand, and
as someone who can't speak, I'm now the quietest person in my
house. Foreigners brush each other's shoulders, like brushing
off feathers. If I lose the deeper meaning, would I be able to fold
my wings, leave my house, and get to a new house? Outside the
window, it's snowing, snowing. As the only person in my house
who's lost a house, I drink a cup of tea, like the foreigners do. A
soft steam. A soft missing.

Blank Notes

How about adopting a fully grown girl? Says a broken-headed doll. The dyed-black lace flaps. Talks with its mouth shut. I wonder, mutters a broken-armed doll, arms crossed. Wire showing through the puff sleeve. A girl can't be fully grown. A girl hasn't grown, won't grow. The broken-headed doll and the broken-armed doll talk. Not the girls I've seen, anyway. In the abandoned box, earnest ventriloquism continues. Even though at the time we could move our phenomenal bodies outside the box. Every time we speak, pieces of plastic fall from our heads, from our arms. When they adopted us, the girls named us. Remember? A name is a name if we remember. The broken-headed doll's lashes quiver. Damn. What am I supposed to remember with half a head? Someone steps on the wire sticking out of the box. The left-tilting doll's arms are a mess. If I could cuddle you with my one arm. If I could inch closer to you by coming undone. Girls gather in the alley and talk without moving their lips. It's possible to do if you clench your stomach, as though to keep from crying. A conversation so quiet that it's beyond anyone's understanding unless someone writes it down. The girls come here and talk like dolls, pausing their growth. Touch one another's heads, dress one another's arms in gauze. What was your name? The girls look into the box. Try to put together the broken joints. They fall apart. We should have adopted ourselves from the start. Ever since we were born, there hasn't been a good opportunity. The girls peer into the broken mirror where words have gathered in a cabinet. By exchanging looks, they have a conversation.

A Romantic Seat

He's sitting on a sofa. Crossing his long, beautiful legs. I'm looking. I'm standing. Is this the basement? He's been sitting so long he's become the basement. Darkness makes me warm. I've had the thought before, that darkness was round. To shatter it, I have to stand up. I'm standing in a corner. Can I feel its shape? I'm standing in the air. A stone falls out of the round ear. I'm standing nauseous. The strength that is required for basement support. He's crushing, crushing his beautiful legs. Sitting down. He can't stand up. A stone comes out of a leg. We've met for the first time in ten years. He walked around some and came back. I was sitting in the last corner he walked to. How much walking does it take to meet each other. A vivid fog rises from his legs. I'm standing on the dirt he spread. It smells nice and familiar here. Before standing up, he sat down for a bit, and the seat was dark and round. From the seat, nauseous, I roll off like a stone. On the sofa he watches the wreckage. Walk all you want, there is no house that is a house. It's because we don't have a home that we give everything we have.

Brewery

They say a house too old becomes human, but the old woman
goes down to the basement sometimes. The place is packed with
rained-on barrels, slices of pork are rolling on the floor. Why,
the legendary world of a bountiful basement sometimes feels
real. She runs a finger over the rainwater gathered on top of
the barrels and tastes it. What's this sensation? This flavor that
dyes her hand as though her hand were wrapped in a blood-
soaked towel. Taking a well-honed blade to the pork, she begins
to laugh. Once, she believed the dark and crimson represented
the sensation of love. Even as they rotted, they were tasty. The
cool pieces of flesh that had been hiding inside her jar-shaped
skirt. They were happy to be ground up and dripping to the
floor. Each time she did this, her basement broadened. When
she went down the stairs and kept going down and out without
stopping, the pigs that had been crying became her sturdy legs.
Once inside, you can only go inward. Like the sweet barrels
growing ripe with agony. The old woman is aware of the fate
of cruel invasion. That crying while holding her breath tends
to ripen very quickly and will inevitably grow deeper. That no
one wants such a thing to happen. That a house rises inside a
person, and that it will often be forgotten. That the house is so
far away that it collapses like a dream. That a person can only
walk to another person if she destroys the house. In the base-
ment, there are souls who have stopped walking, and they drink,
exchanging breath with each other. The fishy smell of blood,
coming either from the rain or the tears, spreads out. This must
be love, she once thought. The souls falter and collide into each
other. The old woman who pops open a new barrel is a person
who delves into the legend of a sweet basement in a country
village not on any map. A person who writes her will in the thin
strand of light coming in through the obsolete window. How do

you expect her to become a fossil in a basement that's too wide to walk across? She's getting as large as a large mansion. In the garden, trees that have endured a thousand years grow down into the basement, and the barrels continue to swell up. I want to visit this lucid forest in the north.

The Winter Lumberjack

When you went into your room alone, I didn't come out of the
alley When you said everything in an empty place and said
nothing in the end, I was in the alley getting hit and run I lost
everything I didn't reach out to anyone I was afraid to be re-
fused I saw a one-eyed person while loitering in the alley An eye
pressed up to a tile and slowly falling to the floor, your profile
was a dream another person needed to approach and complete
What do you mean? you shouted from inside the room, bang-
ing on the door, and the bricks were one by one bruised Like a
sheet of plywood that comes off in the wind, you broke thinly
My day is a side, a facet poured out from the night's many pits
Piled on in the alley are the nastiest things Gunk gathered in
my eyes in the cold wave, and I thought I should wake up from
reality When you rubbed the frost off the window from inside
the room, to get the time precisely right, I was outside falling
into the bottommost pit The hammer was too heavy What time,
what kind of time, is it now I undressed, breaking into cold
sweat *If you cry again and again, does that mean you can start
over?* Am I, to you, a terrifying person because I have two eyes
I picked up the nail from in front of the door You put one eye
to the gap in the broken door and looked at me Don't let me say
anything I now want to build a house that allows someone else
to enter You pressed your swollen lips together I stacked blue
bricks outside the room I began to change into the coldest wind

Arson

If we could deepen and burn and blacken, would we light the fire now? She rests her hot forehead on my heart. Look, the sounds are so deep they're causing a cave-in. I'm holding a candle firmly in my hand. When will the night's whirlwind end? I've been dumped into the strange weather in which the fire keeps getting snuffed. How the breath moves in and moves in deep, should we light the fire before it's snuffed? Before it snows white. She extends her already melting hand and feels for the inside of my heart. What are all these wet things doing in here. She speaks like a liquid. A feeling of flowing down. The dripping wax, is it fire or water? The matter she litters while rummaging inside me. The matter that's glowing in the middle of the night. Through the window, fat snowflakes are falling in. Heavy, terrifying things are falling, falling to the floor. Say we can get out from within the snow, then can this party begin? Say we escape the depth and become lighter, take off our shoes, our clothes, and our crushed selves and float around as very small particles. Whenever her matter seeps in, I grow wild white hair. I hoard candles. To light them on fire. I gather my two hands. I remain in the whirlwind and continue to be thrown away.

Suicide Technique

The women only sprayed hydrochloric acid because they weren't aware of the proper method. Dawn is filled blue with eggs. Enough, now. The women don't know exactly how to kill the babies born every month. They open their bellies to find only crumbling bread.

Hand in the sling, they grab the babies' bare feet and knock-knock on the cement wall. The girl is forever coming to a stop. A black dog licking the glinting egg white. Her tail in her mouth, the girl goes round and round.

Big sisters measure the temperature in the alley on their palms. Whenever one of them steals someone else's clothes and eats someone else's cheese and becomes an adult, the city's only hospital is bursting at the seams. In the hour after the cannon blasts have stopped, the joyful boy of yesterday joins the boy of today and pays a visit to the hospital.

The night after the failed suicides, they catch their faces falling from acid and place them on the girl's head. Beyond the sand hill, what remains of the war are many, many girls crawling toward the forest in the distance.

The old spirits nibble at the thick hands and feet of the children born of the forest. If that were the end of it, those women would open their bellies again and have another look. The empty acid bottle rolling at the lip of the forest hasn't yet managed to burn the girl's pubic hairs.

Young soldiers march past the hospital, to where the city ends. From the persistent itch in the girl's waist, a blind beast has stuck its head out.

Book Club at Night

She marvels at humanity for inventing a room for suicide. Fol-
low the manual, and you may die any way you wish. We're a club
whose strange conversations begin with an illness of the heart
and end with an illness of the body. No one has names, but
each one's insects gather on the table. The hard shells shine, so
sometimes we look at each other, then we close our eyes. Some-
times we muddy our hands. They say those who use their hands
a lot were born to console themselves. Even when you're ill, they
say, short and stumpy hands will beckon other illnesses. Some-
body's hands built a room for suicide. I only want to write about
oddities, says the person whose hand is in the dirt, pulling out a
clump. There are times when the insects fall off the impeccably
clean table. By reading books until she couldn't see, the woman
gained a rare disease. I'll be writing poems, she says. She who
went to the doctor whose résumé had nothing but a name to
show is at the core of the gathering. How should I fall, to contin-
ue the procession of insects? An obsession over death is proof
of wanting to live, and childish. But I'm grieving on my own.
This gathering is turning childish because of me. I want to tell
those children who want to be good people that they're already
good living beings. In the middle of smiling at something I said,
she puts on her sunglasses. First, I have to think of how to write
the manual. Her hands are buried in the dirt, and I've buried my
eyes in the wall, so you, who wrote too much and made every-
one ill, you're the problem. She tries smushing my slow-moving
insect. Let's stop gifting and receiving empty books. The longing
to record does not belong to the eyes and hands. I slip into my
long-neck boots and walk across the table. I like boots. My legs
hurt, and I love to take walks. The one who has abandoned her
sculpture to see if she could hold a heart in her hands is staring
at a bloody lump of light. How do I write only what's odd? And

this, how do I sculpt this? The sculptor mutters. You're a good dirt, I say, walking over the sculptor's lump. The woman at the core of the gathering realizes cold light is entering her now-open eyes. Being ill and recognizing other illnesses is sadder than anything that can be imagined and makes for a sturdy set of crutches, we say, and we open our blank books. There will come a time when only the insects die. Only the slough survives. What do I write in the manual for the dead who want to live? You can't get those crutches by hunting.

Pillow

Down in this sewer, have I become my friend? By the manmade waters where my school principal killed himself, geese cried. On the other side of the barbed-wire fence is a large cloudchimney. I put on a straw hat I picked up in the gutter.

When the clouds bent over, the geese cackled their beaks wide-open. The cry of the machine as it pushed the clouds through the conveyor into the chimney. How come I don't come across better suicides?

My father built his house on the waters' edge, and every day he packed the clouds in, spun the machine. Those who wanted to sleep bought Father's pillows. All night, eyes peeled, I bent my body and straightened my body, over and over. Whenever the bones rattled, I escaped up to the chimney. I thought about what kind of crying to do.

On evenings, I urged him, let's go where there's a crowd, but the geese were bleeding in the machine. For a good night's sleep we need wet feathers, said Father. I sucked on my lips while counting the tags for the pillows. I believe the essence of those who died better deaths must go to the sewer, where innumerable sleeps flow.

When spinning the cotton machinery, I wore my hat. White feathers rose from the waters where those who killed themselves lay face down. I took my hand, stepped on the feathers and went to school in the mornings. Waddling, I forged ahead.

Flesh &
Other Shelters

RACHEL ELIZA GRIFFITHS

RACHEL ELIZA GRIFFITHS is a multi-media artist, poet, and writer. Griffiths is the author of *Miracle Arrhythmia* (Willow Books, 2010) and *The Requited Distance* (Sheep Meadow Press, 2011). Griffiths' third collection of poetry, *Mule & Pear* (New Issues Poetry & Prose, 2011), was selected for the 2012 Inaugural Poetry Award by the Black Caucus of the American Library Association. Her most recent full-length poetry collection is *Lighting the Shadow* (Four Way Books, 2015), which was a finalist for the 2015 Balcones Poetry Prize and the 2016 Phillis Wheatley Book Award in Poetry. In 2020, she was selected as the 2020 Stella Adler Poet-in-Residence. Griffiths is also the image designer for the libretto *Castor & Patience*, written by Tracy K. Smith and composer Gregory Spears, which will premiere in July 2020 at the Cincinnati Opera House. Her most recent collection of poetry is *Seeing the Body* (W. W. Norton, 2020)..

IN MEMORIAM

Mark Pray (1963-2020)

Ronald Lockard (1949-2020)

Carolyn Moon (1947-2020)

C. T. Vivian (1924-2020)

John Lewis (1940-2020)

Stephanie Borges-Griffiths (1951-2020)

Fever

I burn in the frame of me, leaning against dark beams of bone. More or less, I have become a woman I have looked at all my life, standing inside of frames, fictions, lies, or lives where we burn, flame, ash, rage. I thought that loneliness would make me immune to certain consumptions. Instead, my body is consumed by panic, by a crowd of possible endings. Thermometer, Tylenol, Ice showers. This is the awful attention I must give myself. I want to step out of this fever that makes me burn. One hundred & two & rising. One hundred & three. My body leans against its glaring heat. I remember how sometimes a woman glared at me from her country porch, the stained windows of her eyes, her seat on a public bus. I would tilt my head toward the shadows of such women. Even from distances, miles, memories, I sensed their fires, however mute or bold. From the blur of train windows, I see her charred eyes narrowing in recognition. What I liked most about these women was not their faces but that they were *moving*. Even against a page they tossed clods of sentiment and syntax over their shoulders as they clawed their way up to touch me. One hundred, sweet Jesus go down. I lick ice like I am licking the body of a woman I want to put out. I want to put myself out. I am in the teeth of my temperature. One hundred & sticking. I think of how tired spring must finally feel. My body is trapped in New York, in the year 2020. I can't leave these shelters I dream. There are laws. The unobserved ecstasy of silk bursting from buds & what salt remains after, what moves off & under the body's unbearable pink shadows. How a woman can be *going* & be *gone*, aware that even her glare can be an unlit matchstick. Alone, in the shelter of longing, her wild observation can cut its dark silk.

Silence

In another draft I hadn't realized that wherever I'd intended to write the word "sound" I had dissonantly, written the word "wound."

There were such phrases:

The wound of the city is muted inside of blossoms. The nearby wounds of the bus, of delivery trucks, of the madmen shouting on the sidewalks in the middle of the night have died. The men need to be shaved but cannot have their usual razors. The wound of banter in barbershops will return one day and the beards of men will sigh pleasurably in a way men do not sigh elsewhere. The wound of the city makes me whisper in the face & fear of being overheard by death. The wound of the virus is not quite solitude but isolation—isolation of wounds, of the body as a cell, thus cellular, & even the wound of our voices carries in it something that blurs between speech, scream, soliloquy, & siren. The ticking of the wound. The wound of emergencies, the urgent havens in which the mind crawls cannot be touched or described. The wound of immediate transformation time, touch, intimacy. The wound of hours turning their hands against my feverish cheeks. The wound of solitude scrubbing its hands in terror. The wound of my voice in the face of the voiceless dead who are stacked in refrigerated trucks only blocks away.

Only looking back to "correct" this accounting do I see
what the body already knew in truth—

My fleet of fingers flying through the alphabet of sound & wound.
The breaking of the brink arriving, unobserved,
by the bone of the mind.

Flower

I was desperate for blooming. I walked along
city blocks as the lack sunk, depressively, into me. This
was not Mrs. Dalloway's desire. This was not Rimbaud's
gorgeous disavowal. This was a plaintive mewing, a privilege,
a choice that would be denied for weeks. *I can't have flowers.*
Where were the fleets of flower sellers? I wanted brazen cuttings
for my tables, my sills, my nightmares, my comfort.
I read a story about a woman who places daffodils,
or yellow flowers, on cold, zipped bags containing
contaminated bodies. I give up coveting my need
for flowers, how I have never taken flowers
for granted in the same way I have never taken
pleasure for granted. When flowers fell from abandoned trees—
spring in New York this entire time—I stood under trees alone.
In horror, I looked up through the city's gasping.
Indoors, my face was smeared with sick-sweet light.
I pulled pink or white petals from my hair, placing their tongues
on my tongue. *The taste is as indescribable as the world.*
The old comfort of flowers was uneasy inside of our new world.
Our new orders mocked pleasure. Let me be mocked then.
The flower stalls along the avenues I dreamt of
were cemeteries. The men who once smiled, pruning
& arranging my pleasure have gone off
to the business of themselves. *What is my business now?*
In my body the virus bloomed. I fevered. I vanished.
The taste of city petals stuck in my teeth. Bits of petals
like baby teeth lost in the dark coils of my hair & my desire.
The stems & thorns of language is the only pleasure
I taste when I don't taste my fever.

Gallery

Without instrument I make images. My hunger for memory is framed by panic.

How can I remember these shuddering days where hours flicker, dragging me, image after image, against my will? Is that what's happening? A remembering, a dismemberment & disordering of my flesh. Day after day there was rain. Each rainfall filled with the names of the dead. They died alone, behind windows and doors. Inside of walls, they died. Some of them had been dying long before but believed it was their work.

During the days of my fever, I once pick up the phone because I am going to call my mother to ask her what else, what else please help me, can I do, besides gulp ginger ale, to bring my fever down. Oatmeal baths? Castor oil, apple cider vinegar, and to ward away the cough do I need to apply Vicks to my throat, my chest, my upper lip? The memories of her thrash in my chest. She taught me how to save myself. My head turns it darkening, hot clock against pillows encrusted with my bitter sweat. I'm sweating pictures, memories. Image by image, I reach up through the poison inside of me. My mother is going to call me back, I say. My mother has been dead for six years. Jesus. My eyelids are caked with salty deposits of faith.

Will I come through this if my body does not come with me?

I square myself inside of the square bed, taking comfort that inside my head my mind is viral, is the brainy nest of the phoenix rebuilding its wings. I can burn but I will return. I will return with the image of burning. The panic is who will ever touch me again, who will know the taste of these scarlet agitations I have held against my eyes?

I promise my body that my pictures have taken much more of me, taken much more from me, than I have ever, wide-eyed witness, given up.

They died in the images that were not made of their deaths. They died in protest of the living deaths they were told would save their lives. They died, faceless, shrouded in black, plastic trash bags. They died under hands that tried and tried to crack their chests open and draw the poison out. They died breathing the country that failed them. They died without the hands that should have held them at the last breath. They died in nobody's arms. They didn't return to homes they could never own. Beneath florescent lights the sun and moon missed their faces but kept vigil.

My god, I have given up the former world with no need of further vision. If it is not me who is pressing the mechanic button of this instrument, this sweet flesh, if it is not me who is making me, then it is memory, finally, going ahead of me with its face against the earth.

Flower

During spring, this is the only poem I will write:
Flowers for Tanisha
Springtime, New York, 2020

Thank you for the daffodils you leave
on the black lids of their bodies. Each yellow prayer
vibrant in its fading. Each flower clinging
to the flower of the body. New York,
I can't bear your suffering while flowers
burst. O city of my bursting, of my heart, O body
of lonely flower & darker musicals of loneliness.
New York, get up. Tanisha holds flowers in her arms.
I can't afford to live without suffering. The city
is coughing flowers. We come through the rough
mercy of our bodies. We smile behind sky-blue masks
that make our voices taste sick & hurt. There's a man
on Third Avenue singing into his hands where there is bread
or birdsong or his mother's eyes. Maybe he is holding one
of Tanisha's daffodils & in this poem his fever will not kill him.
His song bursts like horns & hands & pots that roar
each evening at seven o'clock. New York, of dreaming.
New York, of shining. Park Avenue magnolias, don't go.
Tanisha's gathering daffodils for body bags. New York,
return & return. New York, ever & ever ours.
I can't bear ghost avenues of neon. I'll stand
on Third Avenue singing to the sun. My face open
& clean as the tears in Tanisha's eyes. Tell her to go home.
I'll sing our city electric with my voice. I'll cry green rains.
O city of blossoming against dead flowers. New York,
do not cry alone in your trains, behind windows. Hold joy,
hold park & hospital. Hold doctor & child, beloved
in the unbroken mouth of our power. Hold deli & rooftop

& slow summertime in the river's trembling distance. Hold
coffee & crowds of angels sitting on Village stoops
& looking fine for no particular reason. O city of our bodies,
heal & survive our hunger. O city, come laughing again
inside of our dreams. New York, the world after you is now.
I would like to believe this poem is a daffodil
placed on the lid of a language that is trying to speak
about the world. Let this poem be a stinging like beauty
in our eyes. O city, we are living on our knees.
Let Tanisha put her flowers down into the earth. New York,
I want to save you. We, who smile in block gardens
of memory where life shines like water on green vines.
We, who love because we listen to the old song.
We, who love because we dance in our living rooms.
We, who risk ourselves by loving
the faces we once touched in the name
of life, & remembered how to take the train home.

This poem is dedicated to Tanisha Brunson-Malone, a forensic
technician in New Jersey, who places daffodils on body bags in the
hospital's morgue and refrigerated trucks that hold as many as thirty-
eight bodies, at the Hackensack University Medical Center.

Fire

We aren't going back that way,
We burned apart—we lit ourselves alive.
We aren't going back this time. We will breathe.
Democracy is a ventilator. Elijah
McCain played the violin. Christian
Cooper watched birds. Ahmaud was running
For pleasure. Who do you think the suspicion is about?
Get back. Grow Black. Burn the civil skin
Of unwelcome settlers enslaving declarations,
Selling cargo, imaginations & vocabularies.
Say community. Say collateral. Say Breonna
Taylor's murderers are (still) free.
George Floyd said *Momma.* That man said
They're going to kill me.

       Watch:

                                They're going to kill me.

Farewells

I sit on a porch where there is a wide brown pond, which has been my view all week. It is July. In the evening there are lightning bugs, frogs. There are four, twenty-four-year-old carp whose dark gliding bodies are visible from the porch where I read, dream, & write nothing. Days that I have been here in the countryside to visit my family I stand apart from my infant nephew, unable to touch his soft, shining face.

When my father arrives for meals, I do not hug him. We laugh. Let our elbows kiss in greeting. For my father, I play music— The Spinners, The Whispers, The Isley Brothers, Sam Cooke, & Stephanie Mills. The good-time music nearly veils our horror, our fear that even should we mind each other, we could all be lost. In the name of love, touch could take us away. We eat fresh crab cakes & key lime pie. We have lemonade. The ice melts too fast. We breathe slowly, our eyes melting as we stare at the pond where deer approach at twilight.

On Wednesday Uncle Ronald dies from COVID-19. The next day my close friend's mother dies in hospice from cancer. The next day or next, John Lewis & C. T. Vivian each die.

I imagine how families have gathered themselves over thousands of years of wartime. In this war, we have not (yet) come through. The virus rears in sunlight, devouring bodies that will not mask, separate, isolate, listen. The virus is the arrow of the nation's ego. The weapons land, as most of them ever do in America, on the black & brown bodies this nation has marked for easy murder. For my people, it is ever wartime.

Uncle Ronald had rich, blue-black skin. His teeth were white when he smiled. He was always smiling. He kept creases in his pants. His shirts were always starched. He was never not found to be sharp, handsome, & elegant. He was a kind, black man whose death was undeserved.

All week I have watched a great blue heron enjoy fish, light. I watched this creature dry its blue wings in the mornings. Sometimes, its shadowed wingspan went gliding across the hot green grass. I have watched the red-tailed hawks, irritated by their cries of distress.

As I sob, shy deer run off into dark green caves.

The last morning in this beautiful place the blue heron greets me.

The startling blue body floats silently in death on its side, its long
    neck half-capsized
by the small fish & turtles who will slowly pull the heron & its wingspan apart. It floats as easily & as ugly, on the surface of the pond. For most of this day I stare at the body of the great bird that gave me peace during these blurring days. My rage is that it died alone & I don't know

it came to its death. When I walk down to the edge of the water the death is so lovely that I am dizzy. I am selfish. I wanted to believe the great blue heron would go on even after my departure. It was going to be a symbol but now it is only dead & good, wasn't it, the days when distant news of intimate deaths arrived, for me to have seen it alive at all.

This is the natural order. We witness living without seeing its dying, which is happening the entire time. The living is so good & ugly we tolerate the ripples, the wings, the gliding & falling. The country heat was already melting the blue away from the heron's flight. The hawks went off to cry elsewhere.

We animals know better.

All day the three geese stay away, stay out of the water's grief until this great blue elegy is finished. By morning, surely, there will be another abandoned body, as is ever the music of war. By morning, again, perhaps it will be my turn. I will be grief's brief and golden host.

If this ever ends, what will I do with my mouth when it is unmasked? And the words that my voice makes—will they melt at the first lick of unmasked air?

Edge

I no longer describe beginnings. I want to say it began in March but it was surely sooner. To think of the lines we have crossed, the precipices from which we have leapt, from the bluffs where bodies fall like rain breaking over the roofs of those bodies. Lately, I am patient about falling or breaking, about regret. I was broken years ago. Where is the edge of me tonight? Where do I, where must I— end? The city is at its edge, or it is in the comma of its common breath, or how can we breathe inside of nights that are so hard to touch? Where is your life inside of these nights and their unlit houses? Can your hand find the edge of mine? My hands are too soft for my liking. I dream that my fingers are made of blue latex. What have I made? Across the immense screens of our bodies, our aching is involuntary. Do not let me waste my softness at the abominable brink. Sooner or later I will tend the edge of the edge with care. Latitudes of earth & loneliness. Alone together at the brink. The brink is not identical beneath our masks. Your mouth is as singular as the lines of your palms. Your mouth is as wide as your mercy. Your begging mouth—*when will this end?* Do you mean the world or did you mean desire or was it something else? The brink shivers. Here, you must touch me—if only in the mind, if only in this city of a dream where petals drift across abandoned avenues & madmen, unshaven in their blues, cluster outside of churches on corners where they will scour the air with curses. *"We will each die. Motherfuck this hunger. Motherfucker can you breathe like God. Girl, you giving me a dollar & can't give me something else? Beautiful, we all out here dying & don't it feel good. Bitch, I look homeless to you? Girl, a dollar ain't going do me no good today. Baby girl—all them fucking shelters is closed. I ain't never been homeless cause I got God in me. You too pretty to stand out here crying on the corner. What kind of dog is you walking? Don't come near me trying to help me. America been helping my*

Black ass ever since I was a itty Black boy & Look. How they going to call something a 'shelter' and then close it?" I go back into my body carrying the words of these voices. I unwrap the words & write them down, unsure if the paper will break apart. None of them were wearing masks & when they laughed & shouted—they breathed. I don't know where they are now but here are their voices, wrapped in paper, in foolish language. I was trying to buy them food because I thought they were hungry but realized they were talking about something else. *We will each die.* And how, *how* is perhaps the heavier word. Those prophets covered their faces, their exposed scars, covered their hands & feet. It was spring so some of them had petals & aching in their hair. I saw their broken teeth & the sores in their eyes that gave their minds a burning. When they spoke of God I could see blue wings floating & melting silently on the surface of water that glittered like eyes above a world of masks.

I am no longer capable of describing faith—where it will end & how it would have, soon or later, begun here in this temple of water & bones.

At This
Late Hour

A. VAN JORDAN

A. VAN JORDAN is the author of four collections: *Rise*, which won the PEN/Oakland Josephine Miles Award (Tia Chucha Press, 2001); *M-A-C-N-O-L-I-A* (2005), which was listed as one the Best Books of 2005 by the *London Times*; *Quantum Lyrics* (2007); and *The Cineaste* (W. W. Norton, 2013). Jordan has been awarded a Whiting Writers Award, an Anisfield-Wolf Book Award, and a Pushcart Prize. He is a recipient of a John Simon Guggenheim Fellowship, a United States Artists Williams Fellowship, and the 2016 Lannan Literary Award in Poetry.

"How You Doin'?"

Of course, I would always ask,
one way or another, greeting
my brother, my sister, my fellow
human, to check in on their well-being,
but mostly I used the greeting
as a platitude. But my mother,

who taught me well, Alzheimer's and all,
shows me what was old rings new
to my old ears. Because of her
condition, I find myself watching
TV shows, I never watched before,

like *The Wendy Williams Show.*
Wendy—who my mom now introduces,
daily, as, "that's my girl"—has a greeting,
teaching me, again, an old lesson:
It's not so much what you say,
but how you swagger it. When
she bats her lashes and holds her
hands out like a begging kitten,
she will begin each show with,
"How you doin'?" To which her audience
replies, "How *you* doin'?"

Can you see these strangers crammed in
a studio, much smaller than it appears
on camera, pushed together, asking in unison,
telling millions of viewers, *I'm good,*
I'm here and in this moment,
I'm up for what happens next,

calling and responding to this gesture
of seeing one another that, for once, won't
be forgotten with the noise of the day?

So, when I think of my encounters with others,
who are quarantined, sheltering in place,
social distancing to stay alive, I ask them
and—*is it possible, for the first time?*—
I truly wanna know.

Hanging Out

Between waiting on the mail and waiting to shave, just for
    myself;
between reading for pleasure and reading out of a sense of
    duty;
between a room of one's own and a bed to share with my
    beloved;

decisions hide within me, knowing they must decide.

Amazing how the sun rises as if nothing untoward is going on,
business as usual, "just another day at the sky."
(Even my clichés paraphrase themselves.
Who can bother with details at a time like this?)

And then there's the issue of desire. How unpredictable!
The ways the heart deadens and then wakes ravenous
through long periods with no expressed love in the flesh.

When I feel hampered simply to lace my shoes to go outside,
saying, "Today will be the day I'll make a difference," when,
finally, it occurs to me, *I have some time on my hands,*

I pull it together,

trying my best to imitate the sun, but I fall
somewhere in-between its daily brio
and its burning indifference.

Be Like That

Like a small song, smaller than a scream
in protest, smaller than the bee's stinger left

in the vein of a neck, infinitesimal, but aimed
true, barely more than a vote cast

on a Tuesday. Be no one in particular turning
their ear to listen more closely than they listen

to their beloved, or be the one who wants
to repeat themselves; no one ever wants

to repeat themselves, especially when they take
a chance to speak up. No one hears us,

until someone points to the smoke
in the distance, rising from the fire.

They're all too distracted by astonishment.
See, the work is telling all the

somnambulists to wake up. The work,
see, means giving it to them direct

but slant, like a slap coming out
of nowhere. You hear it, look to see who

screams, surprised to find it's you,
mouth open before the howl. The hard truth

is what I'm trying to put down, if
you can pick it up: The world cares less

than you think about what you think;
we're too busy being heckled from above, so

we're worked up. Life got as urgent as the cost of life.
Urgent like water breaking inside you.

So folks got mad like when some fool
calls you out your name.

Every fool on the street turns to you
for an answer, but you tell that fool, *whatever*

your mama didn't teach you,
I can't help you with. Some lessons

you have to live through for yourself.

"I move beneath an evil sky"

Today, as I walk around, girded and wary,
I not only celebrate life but I also feel guilty
For living, beating out a tune within my head
To quiet the clamor on the streets. With lives
Put on the line—some just in chance encounters
With uniforms, some with intent encounters
With uniforms—buying a loaf of bread for dinner
Tonight turns into a rebellious act. This care
I offer myself, comes at a cost, but so
Does selfless love, a farandole of protest,
Breath to breath in uproar against
A tear-gassed breeze. Let's face it,

Roethke was right: "This flat land has become a pit."
My love and I, when we were young,
Pressed our bodies against others in protest.
Spit and fire and broken glass made up a day.
But, for now, taking care of one beloved
Can set an entire world free. A new recipe
Changes the light in the room, clears
The clouds passing by our window,
And for one evening, we let that be enough.
We measure time with how our bodies
Move together, an etude we practice while
Cities burn to enjoy—just for a moment, God,
Just for one night!—this freedom we've earned.

Reading *The Tempest* While the News Plays on Mute, It Occurs to Me . . .

I only know what Prospero tells me to know about Caliban,
but like a ship at sea in a storm or Ariel's voice in my ear,
what appears ain't necessarily so. On TV, a young brother
dies, again in police custody; again, a misunderstanding:
the cop saw one thing, but the brother was another.
The stop was suspect, but we won't clear the young
man's name until we hear from his mother. She'll
say what may hold, a true word, uncoiling Caliban's

good name. Caliban . . . Damn, wasn't he beautiful?
I hear Florida Evans cry, *Damn. Damn. Damn!*
And, like that, the spell snaps, as others call
his name. Prospero waves a billy club like a wand,
but the voices keep rising up from the streets,
up from the graves, up from the trees' roots,
drowning out the news commentator on TV.
The volume turns down; the windows
get raised—better to listen, better to clear
the static—this day, this year, of *Now I hear you*
and of, *Oh, My God!   Now I hear you!*

The History of Fear of a Black Planet:
Communiques from Queen Elizabeth I and Donald Trump

There are of late divers black-moores brought into this realme,
of which kinde of people there are allready here to manie.

> What has happened to law and order, to the
> neighborhood cop
> we all trusted to safeguard our homes and families?

God hath blessed this land with great increase
of people of our owne nation, as anie country in the world.

> What has happened is the complete breakdown of life
> as we knew it.
> I want to hate these murderers, these . . .

Blackamoores . . . to be transported by him out of the realme . . .
[though] through their labor they might be maintained.

> I am not looking to psychoanalyze or understand them.
> I am looking to punish them.

. . . whereof manie for want of service and meanes to sett them
  on worck
fall to idlenesse and to great extremytie.

> If the punishment is strong, the attacks
> on innocent people will stop.

Her Majesty in regard of the charitable affection the suppliant
  hathe shewed . . .
in great misery and thraldom and to bring them home to their
  native contry . . .

They should be forced to suffer...I no longer want to
understand
their anger. I want them to understand our anger.

Reasonablenes of his request . . . doth thincke yt
a very good exchange and that those kinde of people may be
well

I want them to be afraid.
I have never done anything that's caused a more
positive stir...

and that the same could not be don without great expence.

Samaria Rice Breaks the Curse of Sycorax

> "I do not lie."
> —Caliban

A guilty plea launches only when options
leave a room, but even that's a chance. They shot
my baby within two seconds—greeted him
with a bullet, before he could say a word.
No introduction, not in any language,
should begin with a gun. Given a choice, I'd opt

for a world—I'd dream, a world—for more options,
one! No telling what he'd do, given a shot.
He was a drummer, a child. Lord, to love him
was to see him, was to *see* him. What's the word

for a mother who loses her child? They shot
the next day out   from days to come. Why him?
As children, (boys) black men first learn a language
of survival when dealing with cops. I opt,

(opted) to teach my boy to steer clear, for him
to play away from trouble, the language
of fear from a black mother. If we opt
for them to grow up fast, to "man up," options

get taken away like years. That's the language
we give in lieu of hugs; we learn to adopt
pain as a child you raise, the only option
to keep him alive out there, to not get shot

out there sitting in a park. Still, he got shot
like a deer, hunted down without a language?
No! My boy's fate cannot be his only option.

"Before you can say 'come' and 'go,'"

"and breathe twice and cry, 'so so,'"
Ariel's words, not mine, but could
any spirit address one of these so and so's,
living between now and hereafter,
as spirits crack and frogs fall from the sky?
We see no more a reason to hope than . . .
No reasonable reason to expect . . .
Well, what more can I say?
That body was once my child, crying
out for air. Dying out for play,
playing it cool, playing it plaintive.
If his body isn't clear enough,
I have nothing left to offer.

How to Celebrate a Revolution

What if…

Say something benign about the weather,
to begin, whether it's raining or not,
just exclaim, *What a lovely day it is!*

using the same inflection with your enemies
as with your neighbors.
Once the sea change comes, people

will prove too bored with disbelief
to argue—surrendering to hope.
At this late hour, when the country believes

it's grown, when twilight teaches the heartland
a lesson about nuance,
we come together to talk

about the news we love to watch,
so we watch another child die muted
on dashcam video; we can almost see

life rise from the child's body
like a silent prayer, floating off
to who knows where.

*

Just the other day, I was thinking
I can't remember the last time I danced.

*

At this late hour, we nearly give up
on one another: We stay home,
we stop making love, we turn

station after station, looking
for the revolution, believing it
will appear on the higher stations in HD.

*

And why, I ask my aging bones, *why
don't you dance?* Struck dumb, I point
to the TV reminding me, daily,

when the music stopped.

*

At this late hour, the reality show
shows our own lives,
and yet we continue to watch,

hoping, still, for life to work out
but not without some drama.
The screen flickers in the dark.

You turn to your beloved, asking,
Did you understand the ending?

*

You stare hard into each other.

*

You go to bed.

*

My people, if you haven't figured it out yet,
I'm talking about how difficult love is
when a country gets involved,

interrupting those mornings when
a mother waves good-bye to her child,
who, framed in the window of a school bus,

waves back. Mother and child both believing
the other will be okay, but both waving gently
behind glass, fearing the other will break.

Later that night, talking about their day,
they listen to each other so closely
they're almost a better world.

When we look out across the city,
into the faces of others, we're
supposed to believe the world was made

big to keep us from feeling lonely.
When we look out across rural vistas,
we're supposed to believe

the world was made vast
so we could run
as far as we wanted

and no one would tell us to stop.
My dear people, my neighbors,
my conveyors of hopes and my workers

of Gordian knots and of chains now broken,
I sow within you like a farmer
who still believes in the harvest,

while the ashes remind us and the births
encourage us and the indolent lounge
under a flaming sky, while the news

carries our fear even as we live it, while
you leave your homes, even today,
to compose love letters and petitions

of yourself in the world, I am staggered
by many acts of hope and the steps taken,
one foot after another, released in this moment

of history carried within you, like a day carries
within it morning and night. Long after today,
we will see a flicker in the mind,

a Polaroid of memory shaken into focus.
Imagine, before the show of your life fills
with static snow on screen, you look outside

and decide—not see but *decide*—there is snow
on the front lawn; you jump
on the white dance floor,

stomping with your boots until
your neighbors come outside to see
just what the hell is going on. Well,

infected by your groove, they unplug, they
join in; we all do, and we continue long into night,
into the coming day, a Soul Train of revolt

lining rural routes, and filling streets
in our cities with our dance.

The Patient

MAGGIE QUEENEY

CAMERON MCGILL

MAGGIE QUEENEY is the author of *settler*, winner of the 2017 Baltic Writing Residency Poetry Chapbook Contest. Her honors include the 2019 Stanley Kunitz Memorial Prize, the Ruth Stone Scholarship, and a 2019 Individual Artists Program Grant from the City of Chicago. Her most recent work appears in the *Colorado Review*, the *American Poetry Review*, and *Denver Quarterly*. She holds an MFA in creative writing from Syracuse University, and reads and writes in Chicago.

The Narrative Arc of the Patient

Start always in *media res*: the Patient before she is

The Patient, crying in the shower, holding a breast.

When uncovering the wound, the gauze should lift

As a page turns, a curtain swells with wind into the room

Where she sleeps in a stuttering shaft of sun. The worst

Occurs off-page. Allow the reader to imagine what should

Not be seen. It should be difficult for her to speak: keep

Her to answers, to the monosyllabic. To whisper.

Confine her to immediate needs: thirst, and pain.

What is not included is as telling as what is:

Her lost hunger, the life before, what could have been.

The simple requests that can be solved, and then not.

Exposition should be kept to the minimum the reader

Needs to know: follow the action. Tendrils of detail,

Remember, taper into air. Lead the reader by eye away

From the page. Every word must do work: Her eyes large

And bright and liquid with tears. The shape of her body

Suggested by the cloth draping the bed. Line of her

Neck. Remember to describe how her thick black lashes

Rest against the fever blooming her pale cheek pink.

Her mussed hair transformed into loose copper tresses.

Everyone needs a character to care for, to be stirred,

And left wanting more. The two resolutions

Available to this kind of storyline: dramatic cure or dramatic

Death: chronic, ongoing conditions present difficulties.

You must usher in an irreversible change. Write what you know.

You must remember the reader: nothing can end in a dream.

Origin Stories of the Patient

Her name, from the Latin, from the French, is not rooted
in pain but her ability to bear. To endure.

One morning, a single cell forked, divided and multiplied.
The Patient was born of a fracture holding a swarm.
The lattice of a crystalline geometry interrupted.

A strand of sand fed into the gleaming guts
of a pocket watch. The particle seed sprouted
the strange barbed arms of a snowflake.

The Patient was born, fully formed, armored, from her own pale
    thigh.

The Patient rose in a plume of plum smoke
billowing out the skin of her old body,
left puddled like a silk slip on the cement.

The Patient walked her old body off, each stride
a shudder, a buck. The ground vanished when
she entered the suspension phase and floated away.

The Patient worried her old body to the bone,
strung her skeleton into a bow, split the heart-red
apple and entered, honed-head first, cloaked in sweet

juice and thrumming, the green wood of an oak.

The Patient was like anyone else. Like everyone else.

You could not pick her out on the street, so totally
the flame of her was hidden, licking her skull
sour in the middle, like a candy. She grew inside

a radioactive bloom, the coal-covered scar scored
by a bolt of lightning, a mountain cave, where as
an infant she grew strong on the milk of a she-bear.

The Patient started each day long. As noon neared,
her dim form shrank, crept underneath the heels
of that other body she was tethered to, her mirror.

No one knows how she broke away. Or why or what
changed. But, like a moon, she swelled into another shape.

Inside the Patient is another Patient, perfect, and one
size smaller. Inside that Patient is another, and another,
perfect. The Patient grows geological inside her own

geography. Her body begs a team of cartographers.
The center of a drab, dun-colored rock. Split in half,

she offers a rough clutch of amethyst, intact and wrapped
tight as a budded bloom. A mine, a mouthful

of prehistoric air, trapped and traveling
toward me all these years.

The Patient Contemplates Quarantine

She hoarded her whole life through.
Mimicking the mirror, she kept her face

Still as still could, never gave anything
Away: the thin long organ of her skin,

A shield she scoured into reflection, to radiate
Out and away. The Patient eats with her eyes.

In youth, she admired descriptions
Of the fisher's wicker basket layered in

Slack silver bodies and sweet grasses,
The butterfly hunter's illustrated guide, and net.

A beetle immortal in the polished bulb of amber.
Photographs of what other women wore

This season in other parts of the world.
She studies the new rituals, commits to the hot

Tap, song and counting, the viral multiplication
Of lather. Now, she covers her mouth. She covers

Her eyes. Nose. Any touch threatens wither,
Contagion, and so she holds her own hand.

Robins chatter, fretting the nest's new weave,
Swell of eggs. She watches from behind the window

Screen as green shoots nose blind ways through
Rain-tacky dirt, swell, then split the tight bells

Of buds into peals, the needling pendants of petals.
All that squander and abandon, a distant ache.

The Patient Delivers Herself

Into the hands of others, their palms slick with

Alcohol or cloaked in latex in a blue chosen

For its quantified calming effect, the color worn

By defendants in court. Eye-color of the heroine

In the story the Patient is not telling, and not in.

In this world, there are two kinds of people.

The body of the Patient poses a question.

Outside the window, spring announces herself

With the tender neon greens and explosions

Of soft blossoms on the branch of the crab

Apple tree, in long, fleshy magnolia petals,

Now bruised and browning over the path

To the front door. Her blood, too, buds

Plum and blushes under the skin. Every mark

Lasts weeks. Appears in her sleep. Tethers her

To these species of tree, their perfume both

Soft and strong as a silk strap, leading

The Patient's body into some realm other

Than her bed. The window glass at her head

Bells, returns to sand. She knows, even in the dark,

Where her hands rest—her first, faithful pets.

The ones that belonged to others, and when.

Through the Procedure, The Patient Learns
Who the Real Enemy Is

The Patient has had rough lovers before. Muscle memory

Remembers what she does not remember. The dark animal

Crouching in the dark of her body. The sharp animal that rises,

Rears. Bucks, then disappears. The slick animal that sleeps

Through the winter underground, deep inside hollowed-out

Trees, or the one that freezes, collapses before a fanged mouth.

The outline of the electric animal thrumming in static the shape

Of the part of her body that was numbed out. On the screen,

Her tissue repeats into strange faces, a blur of landscape

Studies of the moon, its many horizons spreading like milk

Or oil or blood into some unseen beyond. She wonders at this

Need to look. Is it see or be seen. She must ask if it is, finally,

Relief that she feels. To learn the name, and know the home

From the occupant. To trace the route to that mysterious

Elsewhere she can never outrun, and is never allowed to go.

The Patient as a History of Medical Treatment

The Patient takes the cure of water, the cure

Of thirst. The Patient has bathed in cedar,

In pine. She has swallowed whole the heads

Of peonies, towers of lilac, lilies' freckled tongues.

Mornings, she wraps her hair in a net of cobwebs,

Lines her eyes in traces of exhaust left on the sill,

Plunges her hands into gloves of wild honey.

She licks a box of matchheads, chews ice back

Into its mother water, weaves strands of tinsel

Through her teeth. Packs her torso with mud.

Her slick cuirass. Her cracking carapace, she

Lines her skull with velvet, snail shells ground into

A fine, fawn-colored powder. She recites the secret

Images of her last dream, a series of keys completing

A set: what is clenched, crouching inside her

Hips' cradle of bone, what she loses in the hours after,

Running through the stations spelling morning:

Hissing kettle, the boiling pour. The beginning over.

Her body lightens, lessens. Wants more and more.

The Patient Regards the Possibility of Her Own Death

She grew with the distant horizon, its plum bruises,
Veil of rose edged in tangerine, as her oldest, closest

Companion. How the darker outline of her grew out
Of her feet, her legs articulated over floor, waist bent

Into a wall. Her head blended into a tangle of wild
Climbing rose rising on a splintered lattice in the yard

Next door. Her mind formed a simple fork, the two
Prongs saved for meat and pitch, the slick wishbone

Resting over the heart of a rock dove: how will she know
Where to go, after, with no legs or hips below.

How long until every thing she owned is rehomed
Or ground to dust. And then, the galaxies of all she

Touched. The wood slats of the fence, the strip of sand
She wriggled her body into one distant, hot August.

It cannot all be hunted down. The years her body was
An instrument for, not instrument of. Visitor, then touch.

What wild silent rises inside to meet what comes.

The Patient's Book of Saints

The Patron Saints of the Patient are multiple:

Saint of the mercury ticking the thermometer,

Of softness under her tongue; Saint of the blood

Blooming on her breast, her wrists, the tangle

Of red nets caught in the albumen of her eyes.

Saint of the shine caught in the lenses of wild

Animals. Saint of the animals. Saint of thieves,

Of masqueraders. Of wave after wave

Of invaders, the stones they scale, the gate

That bows, splinters, and caves. Of the salt singing

That old song through her garlanded veins.

The one she never knew but hums often.

Saint of cotton and ice and bleach and

Iodine and the slit gown. Of the disposable

Razor that traces the contour of her body.

The Saint of compression. Of the body's

Pull to the gravitational center she will never

See. Of what is left of the course of treatment.

Saint of development, of the experimental

Drugs. Surgery Saint. Saint of the body

That was and of the body that becomes.

The Patient Arranges Her Hair

Before the mirror, she appears
Different. Red rushes to her

Collarbone, collects in a swarm
Or bloom. She swoons slightly,

Wavers like the green wooded
Body of the sapling in a whipping

Wind. How soon her hair splintered
Into a frayed copper rag, face

A flag fashioned from a handkerchief.
There is a hand somewhere inside

The frame, pointing. A river of scarlet
Ribbon belled into a bow of air.

The arrow of her narrow body hurtles
Through the invisible, dragging as its own

Target the force expanding, a diagram
Of a bomb's fallout, a sun's radiation.

The warning she does not see—
Can she still call it warning,

What hibernates inside the gray of her
Limbs, the bones that are no color

Until bared to the light. She steps
Out of her own skin, melted around

Her feet like a puddle of shed dress.
She depends upon the microscopic:

A grain of a grain of a grain, the stranger
Troubling the pattern like a lover, like

A steel pick to the lock of her, her hidden

Tumblers. She listens to their distant falling,
The strange music of all

She has ever known: the boundaries of her
Body, swinging finally wild and open.

Wild Recovery

TRACI BRIMHALL & BRYNN SAITO

TRACI BRIMHALL is the author of four poetry collections: *Come the Slumberless from the Land of Nod* (Copper Canyon); *Saudade* (Copper Canyon); *Our Lady of the Ruins* (W. W. Norton), winner of the Barnard Women Poets Prize; and *Rookery* (Southern Illinois University Press), winner of the Crab Orchard Series in Poetry First Book Award. Her poems have appeared in the *New Yorker, Poetry*, the *Believer*, the *New Republic, Orion*, and *Best American Poetry*. She's received fellowships from the Wisconsin Institute for Creative Writing and the National Endowment for the Arts. She's the director of creative writing at Kansas State University and lives in Manhattan, KS.

BRYNN SAITO, MA, MFA, is the author of two books of poetry, *Power Made Us Swoon* (2016) and *The Palace of Contemplating Departure* (2013), winner of the Benjamin Saltman Award from Red Hen Press and a finalist for the Northern California Book Award. She's the curator of an online project and chapbook entitled, "Dear—" and she co-authored, with Traci Brimhall, the poetry chapbook *Bright Power, Dark Peace* (Diode Editions, 2016). Brynn is an assistant professor of creative writing in the English Department at California State University–Fresno.

Dear Past

I couldn't do it again, that worrying. Time before
our wild recovery, before I learned
my prayers in the gray kingdom, before shelter
was a signal for burning eyelids
and grief tea. Tribes more ancient than memory
walk through you. They wander
the thinnest sky, place between pen and page,
neighbor and trigger, frontline
and garden: whole homelands exist
on faith alone. I couldn't do it again:
all of the forgetting, my spirit fleeing my body
for another present. Do I forgive you?
You carry my grandmothers. I carry verses. Your panic
is almost mine, but I refuse
the enemy's image. Truce is a mask
made of pressed flowers. Daughters unleash
a nation of broken sons. Dear replica
shotgun, dear unroped memory: Did I suffer enough?

Ghazal That Tries to Hold Still

Morning rises like an obelisk. Where does stone find shelter?
The girl I remember plays in her father's garden, a shelter.

Clouds opal the morning, bees make the phlox tremble, sparrows
sing in me as if I were a redbud, as if my arms were shelter.

The ash trees and orange blossoms stand still in midday sun.
Without you, I feel closer to my body's pain. Absence shelters.

Wet nose on my arm wakes me, the dog's metronome of joy
beats the walls. Only yesterday the howl chorus of the shelter.

Have you forgotten the magma, churning at the earth's core?
The animal in us? Rain wakes the sweet bays, the sky shelters.

Like the snail but not the slug, not the opossum but the armadillo
or the turtle's famous comforts, sometimes the body is a shelter.

Early evening, the sun in its thin gray veil. Dog asleep on the sofa,
all bellies full. My mind's skull-bone: an uncracked shelter.

Ghazal with a Box of Wind

Almost music, the red-winged blackbirds and frogs in the distance
trying to summon a season's love before summer's distances.

A single violin singing in an empty square; necklace pearls
scattered over wet asphalt. Hard evidence, love at a distance.

The sound of the door handle, oh the beloved's hands grow
close. The heart opens at footsteps. Even at a distance.

If I could box the wind, the warm dust, the echoing chimes
I'd fold this early summer for you, send it from a distance.

Scarves of smoke purled the grill, laughter sparking the yard.
We hail each other's joy with masks on, keeping our distance.

Night songs: toads croaking, buzzing flies, low-pitched barking.
Poets know how to be alone: holy solitude and sounds in the distance.

The map above my desk measures shipwreck and mermaid rescue
by inches. And you, my friend, are only a thumb-width's distance.

Unstained Ghazal

Roses wilt in late April's heat, a ceremony of blood.
The dog by accident breaks my skin, it blisters with blood.

Rumor has it God wants to love me so much he asked
His son to pay the tuition to forgiveness with blood.

If I could, I'd embrace my mother and father, breathe in
their familiar scent, our lives sheltered by blood.

A spot in the window saved for a caladium—angel wing
leaves, veins stained the shade of menstrual blood.

Whooping laughter in the dark and wind chimes.
I am a ghost in my own house, summer in the blood.

A storm announces itself, but the trees are busy.
A finch scolds a robin, its chest the shade of old blood.

Driving across state lines during a pandemic: Will I be hurt
because of my face, because of what's imagined of my blood?

Untouched Ghazal

Tonight, tonight, the governor decrees we can now touch.
Love is essential travel, the green miles so close they touch.

What's the new stand-in for human skin? I watch
the light glide over the mountain, greedy for its touch.

The anniversary of my mother's death—I take off my clothes
and run and roll and wash and cry. I want everything's touch.

Palm by cracked palm, I press my hands over the knotted
eyes of the aspen. A universe of roots known by touch.

The waterfall trail narrows, the poison ivy awake and glossy.
A family wants to pass. On both sides the risk of touch.

Debussy, Chopin, Rachmaninoff—sonatas ringing
as I gaze down the mountain. The privilege of music's touch.

I can't watch the numbers rise anymore, turn it off.
When it's safe to come out again, I'll know by your touch.

Ghazal Defined By What It Is Not

Only a handful of trees can live here; we live without
sight of the honeysuckle, the ash tree. At 9,000 feet, I'm without

48 shades of green that insist on their own beginnings.
Do the mountains consider the hyacinths they live without?

The day is a sea of moments, each one bewildering.
I want you to touch me, hands I can no longer live without.

I want my shames to be as common as coffee cups, used
and stained by watercolors, not a single secret without

the sun's daily blessing or rituals of doubt. What do I
mean to myself, touched by three, and living without

testing each avocado, missing the ghost heat of bus seats,
wishing for the longing new smiles engender, and without

the stone cup, passed between us? I blend the ochre, the red,
shape the mountain's colors, gestures I can't do without.

Ghazal Seeking Answers

My son wants to know what makes the blue jay so mean.
I tell him the jay's is an average cruelty, the median, the mean.

Your second sober birthday in years; we celebrate
over screens. The storm's shadow knows what this means.

The finch nominates the hanging basket for a nest, a herald
of more spring, but the chrysalis that never opened means

the streets are open and unsafe. Clouds signal more rain,
lightning blinks over the city. I want to know the meaning

of the brainstem, the atlas bone, the flood of hormones
convincing people to fear others. I want to know if it's mean

to go inward, silent, or one way to survive. I am trying
to write you from a wind-sheared house, tell you what I mean.

Sometimes I float my hands around the absence of a body.
Dear friend, it's not electric. Thunder is not what I mean.

The Wounds Are Where: A Ghazal

Her wounds came from the same source as her power,
wrote the poet. Trees brace for wind, open to light's power.

A column of voices rises through the street, fists beat the air
like exposed hearts. Bodies, a risk, always, but also power.

She came home to me shaking and bruised after the protests.
Twenty year later: Her body remembers their power.

Yesterday, I tried to pray again, introducing myself to the silence.
The walls said nothing. My words had none of their old power.

Tough weeds take it: flurry of June snow drenches the heads
of wildflowers. Yellow gems rise, undaunted by the cold's power.

In the mine, we pull them out, one after the other after the other,
sharp as obsidian. Breath is. Name is. An opening. Is power.

Seeking the soul again in seafoam, wounding, silence.
What is the body but inherited stories, the first site of power?

Ghazal That Wants to Be Satisfied

Missing the city and its underground tunnels, enough
darkness there to hide us. Lost in the ruins and enough.

Days and days of rain. Even the double knockout roses
have lain their heavy corollas down as if to say enough.

Unbroken, moaning viola in the middle of a canyon
played by a nameless musician. This witness is enough.

This circle of days, of books, of bread rising, of walks,
of strangers hugging on old TV shows—say it is enough.

Rain washes the mountains, drowns the sun. I grow
a year older, celebrate through screens—just enough.

Yes, this life is beautiful. I've chased its storms, collected
its clouds in a notebook. Stop insisting I say it. Enough.

Ten of wands, two of pentacles, the northern star, forest-hidden.
Your hands are empty cups. This nothing, enough.

Ghazal with an Hourglass

What will I say to my sons about this time?
Waterlines rise: sheer devotion to deep time.

Wounds heal themselves with grass, ice shelves sigh
into the sea, even stars die from their own heat and time.

Reels of stories and headlines, dire, disappear
into future ruins. What threads, salvaged from this time?

I never think about my childhood but keep repeating it.
I save someone I love again, thinking maybe this time

the ace of cups will counter the queen in her cage
of swords. Fortune is a child playing with time.

The future, with her ashes, terrifies, so I refuse
the speculative—my love and I still have time.

Incense smoke coats the verbena and bluegrass.
In the desert, I'm seduced by the mystery of time.

Ghazal with an Identity Crisis

Enough of this modern nostalgia for daisies. I want an ode
to Cretaceous fiddlehead ferns, an epic to poppies, an ode

to limestone, drawn and released by gravity. Karst
topographies birth towers and caves, stones singing odes

to the commitment of bones to the pressures of time,
the open mouths of fossils psalming histories. And odes

to the seabed, its mysterious heartbeat, unthinkable
depths. If I were lighter than water, I'd carve an ode

on a glacier before it calves, let the ice sing its story
before the sea takes it back. If I were nocturnal, my ode

with its night vision would wander with foxes foraging
and hunting the mountain dark. Let me wake with an ode

to garnets stirring their dark beds, a magnolia hymn,
a ballad to valiant hills baring themselves to gravity's ode.

Dear Tomorrow,

I could do it again, watch the heron carry
my grandmother's verses to its despair garden.
I could be a citizen of evergreens and tend
to a homeland of weeds in the forest with something
resembling love. I can accept the patience white
strawberries require. I can learn prayers in the spring
kingdom, can learn from my dog bounding after
the deer that it's okay to believe I carry the instincts
of my ancestors. Yes, there's still a chance for us
both to be tooth and moon and wild recovery.
There's still a chance my last love will not become
my new enemy. Trust me, the faith it takes to let
the violets bruise the yard without slurring through
the grass in panic is almost mine. I can refuse
the image its eager metaphor. I know better now.
Dusk summons me home with its sapphire curfew.
Do you want to know how I do it? I expect nothing.
And then, and then, the bright surprise of your arrival.

Strength

DENISE DUHAMEL

AMIRA HADLA

DENISE DUHAMEL's most recent book of poetry is *Second Story* (Pittsburgh, 2021). Her other titles include *Scald; Blowout; Ka-Ching!; Two and Two; Queen for a Day: Selected and New Poems; The Star-Spangled Banner;* and *Kinky.* She and Maureen Seaton have co-authored four collections, the most recent of which is *CAPRICE (Collaborations: Collected, Uncollected, and New)* (Sibling Rivalry Press, 2015). And she and Julie Marie Wade co-authored *The Unrhymables: Collaborations in Prose* (Noctuary Press, 2019). She is a distinguished university professor in the MFA program at Florida International University in Miami.

Howl

I saw the best minds of my generation (i.e., Fauci, Birx)
    undermined by Trump, doctors hungry for truth,
dragging themselves through inane press conferences at 5
    trying to fix the prez's anger,
angels with hip replacements and fashionable scarves holding
    up graphs, making predictions, scientific dynamos trying to
    break through, to give us light,
who, in spite of political tatters and hollow men, sat up
    Zooming in the virtual darkness of cold hard facts floating
    across cable news hosts' desks, contemplating death rates,
who bared their brains to the WHO under the Elon Musk craze
    and saw Monday Night riots, angels staggering in Lafayette
    Square, flash bangs illuminating,
who passed by unimaginative reporters with radiant cool eyes
    pleading with Americans not to drink bleach—tragedy among
    the non-scholars of pseudo-science,
who were expelled from news conferences by a crazy & obscene
    Know-Nothing, on the whims of a Numbskull,
who cowered in green rooms, undercut, retrieving their
    speeches from wastebaskets and listening to the terrible
    thump of Trump through the wall,
who got their words twisted, regurgitated, returning to Joe
    Scarborough with a plan for keeping nursing home patients
    and prisoners safer, flattening the curve in New York,
who urged the closing of hotels and theme parks, Paradise
    Church, shopping malls with their mannequins' torsos
    glowing night after night
with dreams of capitalism, now a waking nightmare of
    alcohol-wipes, cock and endless balls no longer welcome in
    gentlemen's clubs, strippers shuddering, clouds of debt, no
    spinning on poles, no dollars, Canadian or American, all the
    motionless world of highways with no cars,

Peter Pans playing solitaire on their iPads, plots and more plots
   dug up in cemeteries, drunken, safer-at-home moms and
   dads banging pans from windows and rooftops in honor of
   first responders who were busy at work, their kids home
   from school, storefronts boarded up, blinking traffic lights,
   ambulances but not much else, sun and moon and tree
   vibrations in the spring dusks of Minneapolis and Louisville
   and Buffalo, until George Floyd, until the protests began,
   the best minds of the next generation chanting, demanding
   sanity from the worst King America who was clearly out of
   his mind.

Pandemic Pantoum
—for Debra Dean

In Pennsylvania, Steve's dentist cancels his visit,
says his temporary crown will have to do
until it's safe to open up again.
In Massachusetts, my sister's doc can't replace her hip,

says her limping will have to do.
What is essential? What isn't?
In Massachusetts, my sister can't get her hip replacement,
can't go for a long walk, even with a mask.

What is essential? What isn't?
In Texas, Athena works at Whole Foods,
can't believe a lady walks in without a mask.
And she's pregnant! Imagine?

Athena works at Whole Foods,
the chain where my own doctor shops.
She's pregnant! *Imagine,*
my doc says, *me having a baby?*

My own doctor shops
for formula online just in case
she can't nurse. *I'm having a baby*
during a pandemic! If I'd only known.

In December my sister and I find a formula
to keep my mother safe—a good nursing home.
Then a pandemic! If we'd only known.
Many patients test positive, have COVID-19

in Rhode Island, in this good nursing home.
No family has visited my mother for months
and still, patients test positive for COVID-19.
The nurses dress like astronauts

and visit my mother's bedside for months.
They ask if they can open a window.
My mom says the nurses dress like astronauts
in protective layers so they're overheated.

My mother says, *Sure, open a window.*
In Florida, I walk with a mask,
protective fabric layers so I'm overheated.
It's hard to breathe when it's 90 degrees.

In Florida, I walk with a mask
though many of my neighbors do not.
It's hard to breathe when it's 90 degrees,
dodging people to practice social distancing

from many of my neighbors who do not.
Two people have died of COVID-19 in my building
so I try to practice social distancing.
A maintenance man is in the hospital with it.

Two people have died of COVID-19 in my building
and we have to wear masks in the mailroom.
A maintenance man is in the hospital with it
and the other maintenance staff look scared.

We have to wear masks in the mailroom,
elevators, the laundry room, and hallways
where the maintenance staff look scared
holding mops, their hands in blue latex gloves.

Elevators, the laundry room, and hallways
are now cleaned with hospital-grade products.
Still, I take out the trash in blue latex gloves
then peel them off so I don't cross-contaminate.

I wish I could clean with hospital-grade products.
My Clorox Wipes are almost all gone.
I peel them one by one so I don't cross-contaminate
as I wipe down the light switches and doorknobs.

My Clorox Wipes are almost all gone
and there are no more to be found in stores.
I wipe down the light switches and doorknobs,
TV remotes, faucets and toilet handles.

There's no toilet paper to be found in stores
but I did score some Kleenex on Amazon.
TV remotes, faucets and toilet handles
can also be cleaned with alcohol.

I did score some Kleenex on Amazon
that I can use for toilet paper if I have to.
Purell should be 70% alcohol
to kill coronavirus, though soap works too.

You can use flannel for toilet paper if you have to—
Bust magazine recommends cutting up bedsheets.
To kill coronavirus, thoroughly soap
your hands while singing "Happy Birthday."

Bust magazine recommends cutting up bedsheets
to make your own masks, then Zooming into
your friend's party to sing her "Happy Birthday."
In her New York apartment, she wears a paper crown

she's made herself, glad you're Zooming in to
celebrate. She's even made her own cake.
In her New York apartment, she wears a paper crown
and puts lipstick on for the first time in a month

to celebrate. We friends text her emoji cakes.
Corona is Latin for crown, the shape of this virus.
I put lipstick on for the first time in a month
then close my mouth tight.

Corona is Latin for crown, the shape of the virus.
In Pennsylvania, Steve's dentist cancels his visit.
He closes his mouth tight
until it's safe to open up again.

Strength

I'd started a strength-training class ($25 a pop)
after my mom's hands no longer worked, after her arms
hung weak by her sides and she didn't have the power
to pull up her pants. For two years I'd thought
about the class but was too cheap to sign up
when I could go to free yoga-on-the-beach
which met at the same time. Now, because of COVID-19,
the class can no longer meet. Now, because of COVID-19,
the beach is closed—not only to yoga, but also to walking
and sunbathing and swimming. Not so long ago
I stretched bands across my chest and held balls
between my knees lowering my legs
onto a mat next to other women my age,
some of whom had been in car accidents
or had hip replacements, and others who, like me,
had never thought much about their muscles.
We'd talk about where to get the best Greek salad—
Giorgio's, now closed—or the hazards
of driving at night. My mom dozed
on and off in the nursing home, using all
of her strength, her training to stay positive—
no more visitors, no more Mass, no more matinees—
as she fiddled with her flip phone,
her numb fingers trying to call me.

2020

always sounded to me like a sci fi year
but now it is here with a pandemic predicted
by both scientists and sci fi. Where was I
when I was 20? I'd already been accepted
as an exchange student, taking my first plane ride
to London where I'd catch a train
to Wales. On that first flight, I sat next to a woman
in a shawl—how old was she? It's hard to say.
I remember the shawl looked quite fancy
and expensive. She told me everything would be OK,
that she flew all the time, that she loved it.
Now that it's 2020 I am too afraid to get on a plane,
even with the airline's electrostatic disinfectant spray,
even with gloves and a mask. Back then
I'd borrowed luggage from my aunt, had traveler's checks
pinned inside my bra and a ten-dollar American bill
hidden in my sneaker. Now we are told to use
touchless payments, dirty money no longer
just a metaphor. Twenty years after Wales
I'd be in a bad marriage and would soon learn
Three Dog Night was right. *One is the loneliest number . . .*
And *two can be as bad as one.* Now I am alone
in my apartment, with younger friends who grocery shop
for me because my asthma makes me vulnerable
to the coronavirus. *In the year 2525 if man is still alive,*
if woman can survive sang Zager and Evans
through the speakers of my little record player. Back then
the years started with 19 instead of 20,
when I was much less than twenty, when twenty
seemed grown up and far away. All of my grandnephews
were born in this century. I was born in the 1960s

and soon I will be 60 which once sounded very "old lady"
to me and now sounds young. I was born in 1961
and Madonna is now 61 with a 25-year-old boyfriend.
I know Madonna is not an attainable role model.
I don't have a pool of background dancers
who want to date me. Now no one can really date anyway,
in the old-fashioned sense, though I suppose
two people could wear masks and walk six feet apart
which might have its own romantically charged charms.
I once read an article that said marriage
should be renegotiated every anniversary,
each partner saying, "Okay, I'm game for another year
if you promise to help more with the laundry." Or "I guess
this has run its course, but no hard feelings."
How many years are wasted in bad marriages
as each person plots an escape? What if
you didn't have to wait until that final straw?
What if the initial straw was enough to suggest a pattern
and couples saw it before they really hated one another?
What if the initial straw of a man running the government
was enough to know he wasn't up for the job?
What if we didn't have to wait for an election
to say goodbye? Oh 2020, bring me wisdom
for I am an elder now and need to impart sage
to those around me, those beautiful 20-somethings,
at home where their futures must seem endangered
or working in hospitals ready to save my life.

Barn Babies

In trying to keep its residents safe, the nursing home
suspends all activities. No Sunday mass, no Lifetime
movies with popcorn and juice. No physical therapy
for my mother. No strolls down the hall where she'd
keep a book on the seat of her walker in case she needed
a rest. No rolling into the family room with the curio cabinet
full of teacups, with the window overlooking the geese.
No bingo, no trivia night, no piano bar. And no Barn Babies,
my mother's favorite pastime. She and the other residents
were wheeled into the elevator, then down to the basement
where they could hold bunnies, kittens, and puppies,
where they could pet a diapered goat or lamb, a potbellied pig,
where they could watch the chicks and ducklings peck at food
pellets on the cement floor.   In trying to keep the world safe,
the rest of us shelter in place. In our absence, animals
take to the streets. As I walk nearly empty Florida paths
the chameleons and lizards are out in full force.
In Dania Beach, the next town north, Brian Wood
is making masks from the skins of Burmese pythons,
an invasive species taking over the Everglades.
                                                Mountain goats
roam a seaside town in Wales. Wild deer look into an empty
Samsung store in Sri Lanka. Cows sunbathe on a Corsica beach.
Hundreds of monkeys surround the presidential palace
in New Delhi. A herd of goats runs through San Jose
stopping to eat plants from suburban lawns. Wild boar
and red foxes saunter through Israel, while fox cubs
frolic in a Toronto parking lot. Pumas glide through Chile.
Thai beaches are home to more sea turtle nests this spring
than any time in the last two decades. Penguins waddle

through Cape Town. In Bolivia, horses and llamas
trek a deserted highway.

                And speaking of llamas,
their nanobodies could potentially be used as a treatment
for people infected with COVID-19. When I phone my mother,
a retired nurse, I tell her of this development.
Llamas! she says. *Let me tell the CNA. If llamas are that good
for us, maybe we can get Barn Babies back.*

The Unreturning, 2020

(after Wilfred Owen)

The prez calls us THUGS, has his henchmen hurl
Teargas and flash bombs. Then he builds a Wall/
"Baby gate" around the White House. Appalled,
We adorn it, lauding the afterworld

With wreathes and crosses, signs reading "Stay Woke,"
"I can't breathe." His last minutes, George Floyd called
To his momma. Tamir Rice was enthralled
With his BB gun. Cops kick in bike spokes

Of Brooklyn protesters. Last May, at dawn
Police shoot Dominique Clayton, remind-
Ing us it's not safe to sleep while black. Drained
Of life—Michael Brown, Sandra Bland. Guns drawn,
Tasers zapping, America's vile blind
Spot. This hothouse, this "pushing daisies" chain.

March, April, May

It is with a heavy heart that I tell you that the predictions of the governor and health officials regarding the spread of Corona at our nursing home have come to fruition. Three more residents have tested positive. Their families have been contacted. We are not accepting any more packages but you can certainly send cards. On Monday the nursing staff tirelessly swabbed all the patients on the 3rd floor and others on the 2nd. To date there have been 8 more positive tests. *The latest numbers of the virus are at: 47 positive cases, 5 in the hospital, 5 expired, with 16 staff testing positive. We are talking to many of you regularly to give an update of our sickest residents.*

To date, we have 51 residents who have tested positive for the virus, 7 expired, 17 staff testing positive. We are finding it takes a good 3–4 weeks for people to get through this. *As of this morning we have 58 positive cases, 7 deaths, 18 staff positive. Many residents are showing mild symptoms, but others are seriously sick. We are in close contact with those whose family members are very ill.* We now have 59 positive cases, 8 residents who have passed and 4 residents in the hospital, 20 staff members positive. Please understand that it is extremely difficult keeping up with the volume of calls. We are doing our best to update families.

We are still at 59 positive cases, but now with 11 deaths and 22 staff positive. One more resident's test came back positive making our total 60 cases, 14 expired, 25 staff testing positive. We have been communicating with the Department of Health and we will begin retesting residents who were positive but whose symptoms have seemingly resolved. *Right now we have 62 positive residents, 17 expired residents, 25 positive employees.*

Nine residents who were positive with COVID-19 were re-swabbed and have come back negative. All families were notified with the results of the negative swabs. We, the staff, certainly needed that boost! *To date, we have had 67 positive cases, 18 deaths, 25 staff positive.* Residents have to get 2 negative swabs in order to be considered cleared from the virus. There is usually 7 days in-between each swab. If your loved one gets 2 clean swabs we will be in touch with the good news.

We received the results for 19 negative "second swabs" today. This makes a total of 30 residents who've beat this virus. We got the go-ahead from the DPH to accept packages and flowers for the residents. They have to stay in reception for 24 hours before being delivered to your loved one's room. A belated Mother's Day bouquet would sure brighten the days of some of the residents. *I have been asked many times when visitors can start coming to the facility. This is something that we do not know just yet.*

Police Pandemic

in memory of Rayshard Brooks, George Floyd,
David McAtee, and Breonna Taylor

Brutality can super-spread through infectious viral videos. In
one breath or from one eye-rub, a callous cop can exhale at least
ten viral partisan rants. Each of these situations, unfortunately,
can lead to death.

A single cop can cough up the truth if treated. Due to the
exacerbation of existing (police) forces, vicious participants
from the lower ranks are not often expelled. Interestingly, the
data shows that just 20% of ineffective police are responsible
for 99% of the violence potentially released into their
communities.

We know that almost half of all those with an inferiority
complex—and the majority of those police acquitted for their
transgressions—do not display prior symptoms (asymptomatic
or pre-symptomatic cops). Those police can be shedding
violence into the environment for up to 5 days before the actual
bloodshed begins.

Damnation Nation

Where a prez boasts a "coming-soon" vaccination,
where so many have died because of his machinations.
Where Don refuses to cover his face—insubordination?—
but you don your cloth mask,
                                          your destination
the supermarket, your determination
to find illusive hand sanitizer, your indignation
at the empty shelves.
                              Where, to prevent cross-contamination,
you pull on latex gloves,
                                    but honestly you've felt this alienation
all along, in a country where corporate donations
ensure domination, wage stagnation,
and the elimination of any examination
of your nation's discrimination.
                                            Where a prez's fascination
with sex workers' urination
in combination with inclinations
for his own coronation
is met with our resignation
but not his.
                  Where the detonation
of rape allegations are archived as hallucinations,
#MeToo intonations met with recrimination
and the culmination
of a supreme court nomination.
                                        Where a flimsy explanation
of a journalist's assassination
meets little consternation.

Where the dissemination
of "news" is an abomination
of truth, an indoctrination
of hate, where the impersonation
of democracy unleashes a termination
of democracy, our stagnation
as we face ruination, more procrastination
following our long hibernation.

from During the Pandemic

RICK BAROT

RACHEL MCCAULEY

RICK BAROT was born in the Philippines and grew up in the San Francisco Bay Area. He has published three volumes of poetry: *The Darker Fall* (2002); *Want* (2008), which was a finalist for the Lambda Literary Award and won the 2009 Grub Street Book Prize; and *Chord* (2015), all published by Sarabande Books. *Chord* received the UNT Rilke Prize, the PEN Open Book Award, and the Publishing Triangle's Thom Gunn Award. It was also a finalist for the *LA Times* Book Prize. His work has appeared in numerous publications, including *Poetry,* the *New Republic, Tin House,* the *Kenyon Review,* and the *New Yorker.* He has received fellowships from the Guggenheim Foundation, the National Endowment for the Arts, and Stanford University. He lives in Tacoma, Washington, and directs The Rainier Writing Workshop, the low-residency MFA program in creative writing at Pacific Lutheran University. He is also the poetry editor for *New England Review.* His fourth book of poems, *The Galleons,* was published by Milkweed Editions in 2020.

1.

During the pandemic, I thought of abstract art. Abstract art, the art historian claimed, was the most democratic kind of art because it allowed for anyone's interpretations, anyone's feelings. You didn't have to know anything to get it. For instance, the canvas that was painted uniformly black could be open-ended and be a consensus at the same time. Like a plague.

2.

During the pandemic, I watched the weather. The sky brought forth its clean clouds. The trees put forth their green like store awnings. You could go online and look at places in every weather. I loved best what was ours. Rain so hard it sounded like a crowd. Ours, like a postcard in the mail or the sparklers on a cake. It was spring, a rash season. Then the sun on everything. "The sun never knew how great it was," the architect said, "until it hit the side of a building."

3.

During the pandemic, I fixed on each fear, each fear its own fas-
tidiousness. My mother and the ocean, not even a touch of it,
not even her feet in the tender edge of surf. My friend and the
tunnels he went through with his eyes closed. When we went
outside we wore latex gloves the colors of Easter. We stood
apart in the mandated distance, like the remaining pieces at the
end of a game of chess.

4.
During the pandemic, I followed each impulse as it turned into
a procedure. I bought a can of peaches because I read a novel
in which it figured as a metaphor. I separated the stuff inside
a drawer, like a TV dinner and its neat portions. I looked at
photographs and suddenly understood that a photograph was a
letter to someone in the future. In one photograph, he stands
in front of the cinderblock pattern of a wall, his hair still brown,
his red sweatshirt draped over his shoulder like a bloody pelt.

5.

During the pandemic, I noticed the pencils. One kept a window open a crack. Another held up the tendril growing out of the avocado seed in a cup. One waited on my nightstand next to a pad of hotel stationery. The hotel had been by the interstate cutting across the middle of the map. Driving from one end of the country to the other, I knew I was in the thick of my own story. I looked down to the lit hotel pool. Even though it was late, there were people there, caught in gestures that made me think of Pompeii.

6.

During the pandemic, I knew we were in a period of interval so I considered what an interval meant. The interval we were in was not like swinging in a hammock on a warm afternoon. It was not like making a lesson plan to be taught. It was not even like being inside a car wash and its cleansing tempest. It was more like Lucky's speech in the middle of Beckett's play, its torrent of rage and grief, after which the waiting, which was the point after all, resumed.

7.

During the pandemic, I lost the little lusts that were the sugar cubes of each day. Pornographic lusts. Vending-machine lusts. Ambition lusts. They were now like flowers pressed to transparence in a book of philosophy. I devoured sleep and sentences. "Life is a game and true love is a trophy," the singer sang, all silvery. Who knew what was true now? Death tolls. Or those dolphins returning to the empty canals of Venice.

8.

During the pandemic, I learned the half-hour of sun that slant-
ed into one side of my room, the light like a giant wing. I would
lie on the floor and read heavy books, surprised by the legs of
furniture. The stumpy legs of a stool, the giraffe legs of a table.
On days when there was no sun, I sat there and looked up at the
window, at the sky that was the color of a sidewalk.

9.

During the pandemic, I read a book about glaciation in the Pa-
cific Northwest. I read a book about a composer's life, the agony
that was each of his symphonies. I read a book about moss.
Everything was basically about time. I meticulously dusted
the leaves of my houseplant with a tissue. This was one kind
of time. I imagined where I stood as it would have been 15,000
years ago, the glacier a mile high. I imagined the ice, traveling
through its geology in a luminous round enclosure, as though
the past were science fiction.

10.

During the pandemic, I knew each neighbor by one thing.
The neighbors above, the baby. The neighbors below, the dog.
Someone down the hall, fried fish. Someone else down the hall,
the opera when their door opened. I made my rooms quieter
by standing in the middle of each one, my mind moving in-
tently, like an old man in slippers. I wondered what one thing
the neighbors would know me by. What truth an inadvertence
could betray.

11.

During the pandemic, I had dreams. I gave a lecture inside a stadium with only my voice. I was small and lived within a key-hole. I walked on a pilgrimage trail with my pack gaining a new item each day. I would wake with sour eyes. My sister called to ask what had become of my money. My friend called to ask if I needed groceries. Each conversation was like dreaming in a dream, like being inside an egg's slushy light.

12.

During the pandemic, I understood how far away I was from
things I once knew with forensic intensity. How the French
parliamentary system worked. The tempers of one man's face.
Differential equations. I had time to think of the turn at the
heart of each thing. *Abandon*, for example. That it could mean
free and unfettered in one usage. And, in another, leave behind.

13.

During the pandemic, I listened. Things hummed their tunes.
The pear. The black sneaker. The old-fashioned thermometer.
The stapler with the face of a general from Eastern Europe.
Once, my father confessed he had taken the padlock from his
factory locker and clipped it on the rail of a footbridge at the
park. He had retired. The park was near his house. Each time
he went there, I imagined him feeling pleased, going to work.

ACKNOWLEDGMENTS

STEPHANIE STRICKLAND

"Time-Capsule Contents," "*Jus Suum*: What Can Never Be Taken," "Burning Briar Scanning Tunnel," "Black \ White," "Virus," "Body of Twisted Tangled Surfaces," "Constant Quiet," "Fourth Fate · Spin-Steer / Musician," *How the Universe Is Made* (Ahsahta Press, 2019)

"One Sentence To Save in a Cataclysm," *Talisman*

"Hum," *Touch the Donkey*

SHANE MCCRAE

"Skating Again at Forty-Four," *Court Green*

"The Second Death," *The Rialto*

"I Hear the Wild Birds Singling Tangled Roads," *Together in a Sudden Strangeness* (Knopf, 2020)

J. MAE BARIZO

"Lux Aeterna," *Bellingham Review*

"The Mothers," *Poetry* magazine

"At the Whitney, Thinking About the Trees," *Bellevue Review*

B. A. VAN SISE

All photographs from *The Infinite Present*

JON DAVIS

"The Body is the Site of Discipline," *Bennington Review*

"Choose Your Own America," *Philadelphia Review of Books*

"Ode to the Coronavirus," terrain.org

"Vintage," *Bennington Review*

JAE KIM

"Sister" and "Guest," *Lana Turner*

"Blank Notes," *Guernica*

"Brewery," *The Poetry Review* (The Poetry Society UK)

"The Winter Lumberjack" and "Arson," Action Books, *Poetry in Action* series
    online
"Mama's Marmalade," *Asymptote*
"Roommate, Woman" and "Pillow," *Words Without Borders* and American
    Academy of Poets (Poets.org) ("Roommate, Woman" was one of the win-
    ning poems of the inaugural poetry-in-translation contest by WWB and
    AAP, judged by Mónica de la Torre, and also appears on Poem-a-Day.)

RACHEL ELIZA GRIFFITHS
"Flowers for Tanisha," *Together in a Sudden Strangeness* (Knopf, 2020)

A. VAN JORDAN
"I Move Beneath An Evil Sky," The Roethke Poetry Prize Calendar

TRACI BRIMHALL / BRYNN SAITO
"Ghazal That Tries to Hold Still," *Guesthouse*
"Ghazal with a Box of Wind" and "Unstained Ghazal," *South Florida Poetry
    Journal*

DENISE DUHAMEL
"Damnation Nation," *Columbia Poetry Review*
"Strength" and "2020," *The Common*
"Howl," *Hole in the Head Review*
"Barn Babies," *Mollyhouse*

OTHER TUPELO ANTHOLOGIES

Native Voices: Indigenous American Poetry, Craft and Conversations
  edited by CMarie Fuhrman and Dean Rader

Xeixa: Fourteen Catalan Poets
  translated by Marlon L. Fick and Francisca Esteve

Gossip and Metaphysics: Russian Modernist Poems and Pros
  edited by Katie Farris, Ilya Kaminsky, and Valzhyna Mort

A God in the House: Poets Talk About Faith
  edited by Katherine Towler and Ilya Kaminsky

New Cathay: Contemporary Chinese Poetry
  edited by Ming Di

No Boundaries
  edited by Ray Gonzalez

Another English: Anglophone Poems from Around the World
  edited by Catherine Barnett and Tiphanie Yanique